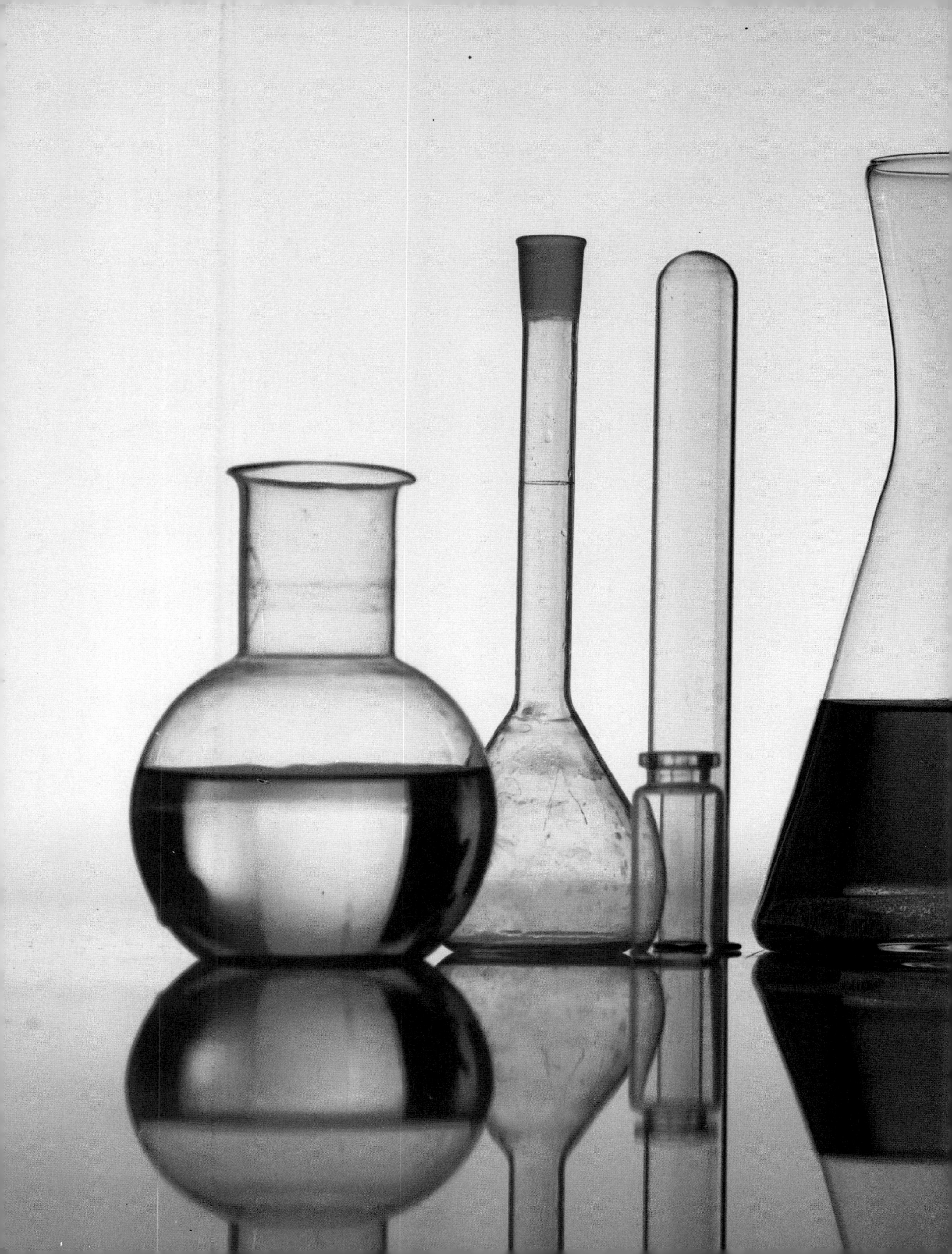

First published in 2018 by New Holland Publishers
London • Sydney • Auckland

131-151 Great Titchfield Street, London WIW 5BB, United Kingdom
1/66 Gibbes Street, Chatswood, NSW 2067, Australia
5/39 Woodside Ave, Northcote, Auckland 0627, New Zealand

newhollandpublishers.com

Copyright © 2018 New Holland Publishers
Copyright © 2018 in text: Stuart Kumar-Terry
Copyright © 2018 in images: New Holland Publishers

All rights reserved. No part of this publication may be reproduced, stored in a retrieval system or transmitted, in any form or by any means, electronic, mechanical, photocopying, recording or otherwise, without the prior written permission of the publishers and copyright holders.

A record of this book is held at the British Library and the National Library of Australia.

ISBN 9781921580482

Group Managing Director: Fiona Schultz
Publisher: Alan Whiticker
Project Editor: Rebecca Sutherland
Designer: Sara Lindberg
Production Director: James Mills-Hicks
Printer: Toppan Leefung Printing Limited, China

10 9 8 7 6 5 4 3 2 1

Keep up with New Holland Publishers on Facebook
facebook.com/NewHollandPublishers

REACTION – happens when different atoms, molecules or chemicals interact with each other and change their structure.

REDSHIFT – the effect where the light from stars and galaxies moving away from Earth becomes more red in color.

SATELLITE – an object that orbits in space around a larger object.

SOLUTION – the answer to a question or problem.

SPACETIME – the combination of all the Universe's dimensions. The main four dimensions are up and down, left and right, forward and backwards and also forwards and backwards *in time*. If you had a box that had nothing in it at all, not even one atom, the box would still be part of *spacetime* and spacetime would still be inside it.

SQUARED – when you multiply a number by itself. Two squared (2^2) is the same as two times two (2×2). Four squared (4^2) is the same as 4 times 4 (4×4).

STRATOSPHERE – the second lowest layer of the atmosphere. One of the important features of the stratosphere is the ozone layer, which protects the Earth from dangerous energy coming from space.

SUBSTANCE – any type of regular matter.

SUPERBUG – a dangerous type of bacteria or virus that is resistant to modern medicines and very difficult to cure or even stop spreading.

TECHNOLOGY – a machine, device or tool created by the knowledge and learning of science.

THEORY – a well-known and commonly agreed idea that has a lot of data to support it and is generally thought to be true. Some theories, like the theories about miasma or spontaneous generation, are now known to be incorrect. Other theories, like the Theory of Gravity, or the Theory of Evolution, have so much data and evidence proving them to be true that they are basically scientific fact. Everyone agrees that they are mostly or entirely true.

ULTRA-CLEAN ROOM – a special kind of laboratory that is completely closed off from the outside world. Scientists control exactly what goes into and comes out of the room to make sure that no contamination can happen. These rooms are used to make very careful measurements or to avoid very common contaminating effects.

UNIVERSE – the entirety of space and time. Everything, everywhere from the beginning of time until the end of time.

VACCINE – a medicine that is used to prevent people from getting disease by teaching their body how to defend itself.

VOLTAIC PILE – the first ever type of battery. Voltaic piles use the difference in energy between metals to create electrical energy.

ORBIT – the path taken by an object as is circles around another object. In astronomy, it usually refers to small objects in space moving around bigger ones. For example, the Moon is in orbit around the Earth and the Earth is in orbit around the Sun.

OZONE – a kind a molecule that is made by three oxygen atoms joined together. There is a layer of ozone in the atmosphere which protects the surface of the Earth from dangerous energy coming from space.

PARTICLE – a very small portion of matter. There are many different types of particles, but they are all very, very small. Most particles we've found are made of particles that are even smaller.

PHILOSOPHY – the study of the nature of reality and the study of different ways to think about the Universe. Philosophy is similar to science. But if science is all about collecting data and making theories based on the data, philosophy is all about how we think and how we make decisions.

PHYSICS – the study of matter and energy in the universe. Physics is all about figuring out how and why things happen the way they do. Physics can be about really huge things like stars and galaxies, but it can also be about really tiny things, like the smallest particles.

PROTON – a tiny particle with a positive charge. A positive charge means that is has an energy that pulls it towards negative charges, like electrons, and away from other positive charges. In the world of tiny particles, opposite charges come together and the same charges push apart.

QUANTUM PHYSICS – the study of the tiniest of tiny particles. Quantum physics is a strange and unpredictable kind of science where particles can come into existence and then disappear like magic, and where you can't ever measure something without changing it!

RADIOACTIVITY – the release of energy and particles caused by unstable atoms.

GREENHOUSE GAS – a gas that absorbs energy and traps heat in the atmosphere, causing global warming.

HELIOCENTRIC – any theory about the Sun and planets that puts the Sun in the middle is heliocentric.

HYPOTHESIS – a theory that has not yet been proved to be true.

JOULE – a unit for measuring energy. It's just like a meter or yard for measuring length, or a gram or ounce for measuring weight.

LEYDEN JAR – a device once used to capture and store energy. Today we do the same thing using devices call capacitors.

LIFT – the force created by the movement of air over a wing that lifts the wing up.

LOGIC – the way of thinking where you make opinions and guesses based on reason and evidence, rather than beliefs.

MATERIAL – an object which can be used to make something. Material also can mean the same thing as matter.

MATHEMATICS – the study of numbers.

MATTER – a physical object of any size that takes up space and has weight.

MIASMA – the smelly gas that many scientists once thought was responsible for causing many diseases. The theory of miasma has now been proved to be incorrect.

MICROORGANISMS – tiny living creatures so small that you can't see them with your eyes.

MODEL – something that scientists use to describe how a science works. Sometimes the thing they are describing is too big or too small to see with your eyes. Sometimes a model does not look like the thing it is describing, but it's helpful to imagine how it works.

MOLECULE – a tiny particle that is made when two or more atoms join together.

MONTREAL PROTOCOL – the agreement that 43 countries signed to stop using dangerous chemicals called chlorofluorocarbons, or CFCs.

NASA – short for National Aeronautics and Space Administration. NASA is the United States government department which is responsible for all its space missions.

NEUTRON – a tiny particle usually found in the middle, or nucleus, of atoms. Unlike protons and electrons, it has no charge. Scientists have found that neutrons use a strange energy called the strong force to hold the nucleus of the atom together.

NEUTRON STAR – a small but extremely heavy space object that is sometimes left behind when stars explode.

NUCLEAR – anything that comes out of the nucleus of atoms is nuclear. Nuclear energy and nuclear weapons mean energy and weapons which use the power that can come out of atoms when the nucleus changes.

NUCLEUS – the tiny amount of actual physical stuff that is at the very center of every atom. The nucleus is made of even smaller particles called protons and neutrons.

OBSERVE – to look closely at something and notice important details

EXPERIMENT – a test used to collect information or prove a theory.

EVOLUTION – the slow changes that happen to groups of animals over time. Evolution causes the creation of new species and the extinction of old ones.

FOSSIL – the imprint sometimes left in rocks by living things. When a living thing dies, sometimes its body can be trapped underground and it leaves its shape behind in the rock. The gap left by its body is slowly filled until a rock is left behind that is the same shape as the remains of the animal. Using fossils, we can know all about animals that haven't been around for millions of years.

GALAXY – a large group of billions of stars that all move through the universe together.

GENERATOR – a device for turning movement into electrical energy.

GEOCENTRIC – any theory of the Sun and the planets that puts the Earth in the middle is geocentric.

GEOLOGY – the study of the Earth. It includes how the Earth works, what it's made of and why different things on Earth happen. Anything that's beneath your feet and not alive is studied by geologists.

GERM THEORY – the theory that very small creatures with the ability to spread and multiply are the cause of many diseases.

GLOBAL WARMING – the slow increase in the temperature of the Earth's surface caused by changes in the atmosphere. Sometimes global warming happens naturally. At the moment, global warming is being caused by humans.

COAL – a kind of fuel that is made mostly of carbon atoms. The coal on earth was mostly made more than 300 million years ago when a huge number of trees was trapped beneath the Earth's surface. The heat and time eventually transformed all the dead plants from that time into coal.

COMPUTER – today we think of it as a device for running programs and making calculations. But before the modern electronic computer, computers were people (mostly women) who did mathematics and other work for scientists and engineers.

CONCLUSION – the summing-up of an experiment where you state what you learned and what you discovered.

CONTAMINATED – when a substance gets something unwanted in it.

COPROLITE – the fossils made by dinosaur poo.

COSMIC MICROWAVE BACKGROUND – the light that is left over from the Big Bang at the very beginning of time, which is invisible to the naked eye.

DARK ENERGY AND MATTER – the hidden energy and matter that scientists can't find or explain in the universe.

DATA – the knowledge and information that is collected from looking at the world and doing experiments.

DECAY – when something falls apart. For radioactive atoms, it's when the atom releases radioactive energy and particles and becomes one or more smaller atoms.

DISCOVER – to find out something new, either by accident or by searching for it.

ELECTRICITY – energy caused by the movement of electrons.

ELECTRON – a tiny particle with a negative charge. A negative charge means that is has an energy that pulls it towards positive charges, like protons, and away from other negative charges. In the world of tiny particles, opposite charges come together and the same charges push apart.

ELEMENT – a substance that is only made of one type of atom. Every different type of atom is a different element. The type of atom is determined by the number of protons that it has.

ENGINEERING – whenever you use science to make something for people to use. Science is about learning and discovery. Engineering is about using that information to make or build something useful.

ENVIRONMENT – the natural world that is all around us, including the air, ground, oceans, rivers and more.

EQUATION – a mathematical statement used to make calculations.

GLOSSARY

AGRICULTURE – any kind of growing and farming used to make a product for human use. This includes farming animals and plants for food, medicines, fuel, building materials and more.

AIR RESISTANCE – the effect caused by air slowing and stopping moving objects. If you wave your hand fast, you can feel air slowing your hand down – that's air resistance!

ANALYZE – to study something in detail and use the information to explain the results.

ANTIBIOTIC – a kind of medicine used to kill harmful bacteria that cause disease.

ATMOSPHERE – the layers of air that surround the Earth's surface. The atmosphere has many different layers. In order from closest to furtherst from the surface of the Earth, the biggest layers are the troposphere, the stratosphere, the mesosphere, the thermosphere and the exosphere.

ATOM – the smallest type of particle that can be used to make chemicals. Atoms are so small that there are more than 5,000,000,000,000 just in the full stop at the end of this sentence. There are some particles even smaller than atoms, called subatomic particles, but these are too small to make chemicals. They are what make up atoms and are only big enough to interact with other subatomic particles.

ATOMIC WEIGHT – the weight of an individual atom. Every element has a different atomic weight, because they each have a different number of protons and neutrons. They have a different number of electrons too, but these are so small and light that they make almost no difference to the atomic weight.

BACTERIA – a simple, tiny living organism with only one cell. The cell is the most basic structure for living things and all known living things are made up of one or more cells. Humans have trillions of cells which all work together to make our bodies work. Most bacteria are harmless, but some can be dangerous and even deadly to humans.

BIG BANG THEORY – the theory that the entire Universe started off all packed together into a tiny space smaller than the smallest atom, and then exploded out into everything you can see all around you. We still don't know how big the Universe really is. Scientists think this happened about 13.7 billion years ago.

BIOLOGY – the study of living things. Any science to do with living things is biology.

BLACK HOLE – the heaviest object known to humans. Black holes are made when the biggest stars explode and then suddenly collapse.

CEPHEID – a type of star that flashes in a pattern.

CHEMICAL – a chemical is a type of substance. In a chemical, we know what all the atoms and molecules in it are, how they are bonded together, and how they interact with one another.

CHEMISTRY – the study of how atoms and molecules interact with one another to make chemicals and other materials.

CLIMATE CHANGE – the massive, global, long term changes to weather caused by global warming.

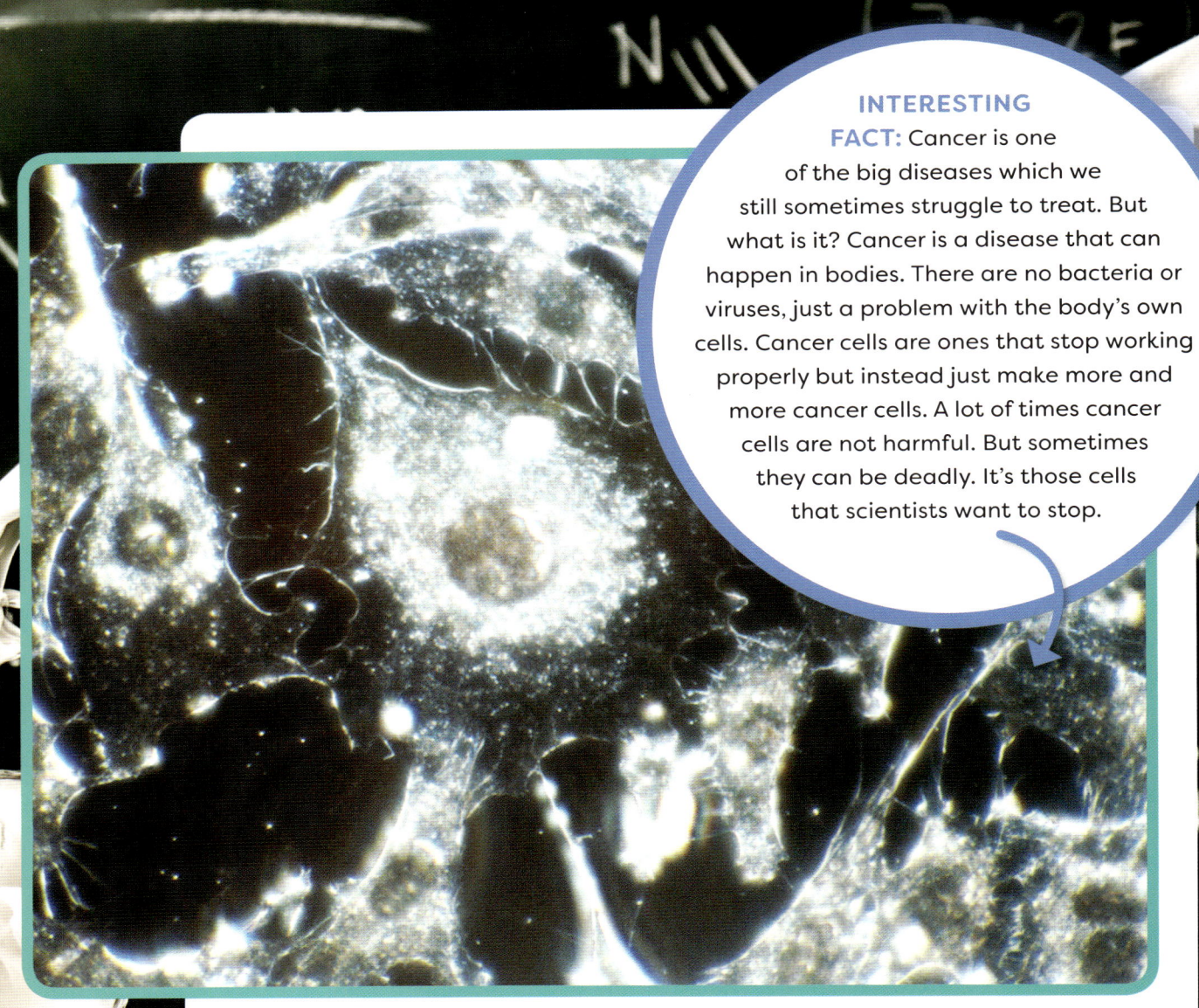

Cancer cells.

INTERESTING FACT: Cancer is one of the big diseases which we still sometimes struggle to treat. But what is it? Cancer is a disease that can happen in bodies. There are no bacteria or viruses, just a problem with the body's own cells. Cancer cells are ones that stop working properly but instead just make more and more cancer cells. A lot of times cancer cells are not harmful. But sometimes they can be deadly. It's those cells that scientists want to stop.

there's a plant, or a fish, or a frog deep in the Amazon rainforest that contains the secret to saving millions of lives. We won't know until scientists can find them and research them.

And more than any of the above, we need science to save ourselves. Scientists have the power to make incredible changes. Scientists can save the world, save lives and make lives better. Scientists can look back to the beginning of time, understand the smallest living things and travel to the stars. Science has made humans what we are.

No matter what you are interested in, there is a kind of science out there waiting just for you, and there are more questions to be answered, more to discover than ever before. Just like Galileo Galilei, Marie Curie, Albert Einstein or Rachel Carson, you too can use the incredible power of science ***to change the world***!

In quantum physics, scientists have found that atoms aren't just made of neutrons, protons and electrons, but dozens of other particles too. We've found things like **quarks** and **leptons** and **bosons** by bashing atoms together at almost the speed of light and seeing what comes out. But how does it all work? How does it fit together? If understanding the atom meant inventing the nuclear bomb and nuclear power, what will understanding all these particles mean? What secrets are waiting to be unlocked?

In chemistry and medicine, there are still millions of chemicals waiting to be discovered. For many diseases there is still no cure or treatment. And even worse, there are thousands of people dying every day from diseases we have cures for, but we can't get the medicine to the sick people. The world needs more doctors and nurses everywhere, to give medicine and to teach people the best way to be healthy, and to research new treatments to help more people get better.

In biology, we are discovering new species every day. More than 80% of the species on Earth are undiscovered. Maybe there's a bacteria out there that can show us how to cure cancer? Maybe

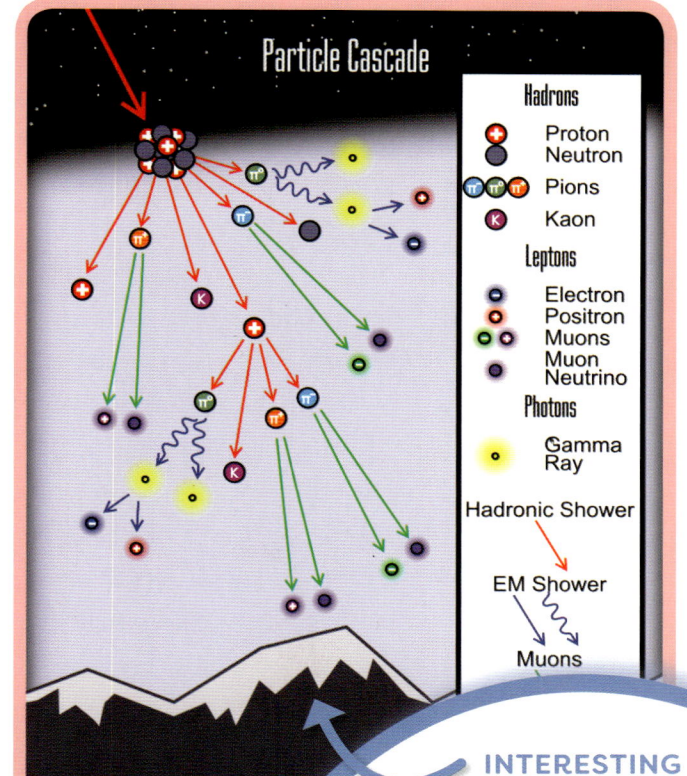

Particle Cascade

Hadrons
- Proton
- Neutron
- Pions
- Kaon

Leptons
- Electron
- Positron
- Muons
- Muon Neutrino

Photons
- Gamma Ray

Hadronic Shower

EM Shower

Muons

> **INTERESTING FACT:** The above picture shows just how many different particles are hidden inside atoms! In this picture a high energy particle called a **cosmic ray** is hitting an atom in our atmosphere. What happens next is just *a few* of the possibilities! Scientists are finding new particles all the time and slowly discovering more and more about how the Universe really works. Will you be the one to discover the particle that changes the world?

In engineering and physics, Einstein's theories say that it is impossible to travel faster than the **speed of light**. People used to say that it was impossible to travel faster than the **speed of sound** too. But in 1947, only 44 years after the first aeroplane was invented, a man named Chuck Yeager became the first person to travel faster than the speed of sound. If we could figure out the mystery of **faster than light travel** we could start visiting distant stars!

In astrophysics, scientists have found that there must be more energy and matter in the universe, but we can't find it anywhere!

They call it **dark energy** and **dark matter**, which sounds like something out of a movie, but really, we have no idea what it is! Who will be the person to solve that mystery? And who will find the next clue to figuring out why gravity works on people and planets, but not atoms?

WHAT'S LEFT TO DISCOVER?

The world is full of some amazing science. Every day we use electricity, drive cars, fly in planes, use computers and phones, and a hundred other incredible things. All these technologies need science to exist. Because of science, we know how old the Earth is, how the Universe began, and where the Earth is in the Universe. Science has made a difference to countless lives, with wonderful cures and life-saving chemicals.

But there is still so much that we do not know, so much more to be discovered!

INTERESTING FACT:
The nearest star to our Sun is called **Alpha Centauri**. Except it isn't one star, it's actually two: called Alpha Centauri A and Alpha Centauri B. They are very close together and make something called a **binary star system**. We don't know if there is a planet anywhere in the Alpha Centauri system, but we can imagine what it might be like. Maybe it will even have some alien life on it?

The world will look very different in 50 years if we don't do anything now, with higher than normal temperatures being recorded around the world – and rising! The North and South Poles are particularly feeling the effects of these changes, getting hotter and hotter. No wonder the ice on the poles is melting!

Of course, there's an easy solution! The main greenhouse gas is **carbon dioxide**, which mostly comes from humans burning **coal** to make electricity. We can stop using coal and switch to using **renewable** energy like **wind** or **solar power** – as long as the Sun shines and the wind blows, you've got plenty of energy!

Now can you guess what happens next? All the people who mine, sell, and burn coal are trying to pretend that global warming and climate change isn't happening! Why? Because they make a lot of money from coal and they don't want to stop making money if people stop paying for it. This has been a major issue for more than 20 years. More than 97 out of 100 expert scientists agree that global warming and climate change are caused by humans. But still, people keep burning coal and petrol and releasing all the other greenhouse gases too.

This could be devastating for everybody. Billions of people could be forced out of their homes and cities by the rising oceans. Heat waves and bad weather can also cause injury and death. Extreme weather can even destroy the food we need to survive. But 50 years after Rachel Carson wrote about environmental disasters, people still don't believe that humans have the power to change and destroy the world.

Hurricane Isabel.

Effects Of Climate Change

One of the most dangerous effects of global warming and climate change is increasingly powerful storms. The worst storms are called **tropical cyclones**, or **hurricanes**. Hurricane Isabel killed 50 people and caused $5.5 *billion* worth of damage. Imagine if you had a hurricane twice as big? Or ten times? Without action, cyclones much bigger than Isabel could happen more and more.

Below you can see a picture of a coral reef. This used to be full of color and thousands of fish and other animals and plants. Now it's just a dead, white wasteland. This terrible process is called **coral bleaching**. Every year more and more coral reefs are being destroyed this way. But what causes it? You guessed it…global warming. Increasing the temperature of the ocean by just one or two degrees can be enough to kill off huge amounts of coral. It could take thousands, even millions of years to get better, if it ever does at all. The environment can be tough, but it can also be extremely fragile. A small change can cause massive destruction.

This, more than anything else, is the reason why science is so important! We need to keep learning, keep exploring and keep fighting for the truth that science reveals, or else we might just destroy the planet.

Coral bleaching.

Climate Change

Today, we are facing the most dangerous and deadly environmental disaster in history. You may have heard it called **climate change**, or **global warming**, but these are two sides of the same huge environmental event.

For more than a hundred years, scientists noticed that the Earth was slowly getting warmer. Then suddenly it started warming very quickly. Scientists realized that we had added gases to the atmosphere, called **greenhouse gases**. Greenhouse gases stop heat from leaving the Earth – so the more greenhouse gases, the hotter the Earth becomes.

That doesn't mean that every day is going to be hotter than yesterday. The whole planet's temperature may only go up by a few degrees. But that is enough to melt the polar icecaps, which makes the sea level go up. It means more and worse storms, cyclones and tornadoes. It means floods in some places and droughts in other places. We call all of these effects **climate change**. Climate change is caused by **global warming**.

INTERESTING FACT: Climate change is a weird thing. It changes how the weather works. The east coast of North America has had some of the coldest winters ever recorded. But the west coast of North America has had some of the hottest summers. It's hard even for scientists to understand how it all works.

Clair Cameron Patterson

Three years after *Silent Spring* was published, an American geologist named Clair Patterson discovered that the air, the water, the soil, *everything*, had an unsafe level of lead. **Lead poisoning** is deadly to plants and animals, including humans. Patterson realized that by using lead in factories and putting lead into petrol, lead was getting everywhere. It was in the air, the water, the ground, and even in people, plants and animals. If it kept going, the whole world would become sick from lead poisoning.

His discovery also caused outrage, particularly with the petrol companies. Why? Because the petrol companies had made a lot of money from leaded petrol and they didn't want it to stop. So, they hired scientists to do bad research which said that lead was fine, so they could keep making money.

Patterson fought for 20 years against the companies and their scientists in courts, schools, universities and the news. By 1986, leaded petrol finally stopped being used. Today, the amount of lead in the blood of the average American has dropped by 80%. Another disaster avoided!

Frank Rowland and Mario Molina

In 1974, two scientists named Frank Rowland and Mario Molina discovered another huge problem for humans. People had been using chemicals called chlorofluorocarbons, or CFCs, in all kinds of ways, such as in the pipes of fridges and in spray cans. But Rowland and Molina realized that the CFCs were getting all the way up into a part of the atmosphere called the stratosphere. In the stratosphere there is a chemical called ozone which protects us from nasty radioactivity coming from space. Rowland and Molina realized that CFCs were destroying the ozone molecules, creating a hole over the North and South Poles that the radioactivity could get through.

Even though CFCs are harmless to humans, they are incredibly destructive to ozone molecules. One molecule of CFC can destroy up to 100,000 molecules of ozone!

The ozone hole is the size of a whole continent – that's a huge impact that has happened over only 30 years! But it may take as much as a few hundred years to be properly close it again.

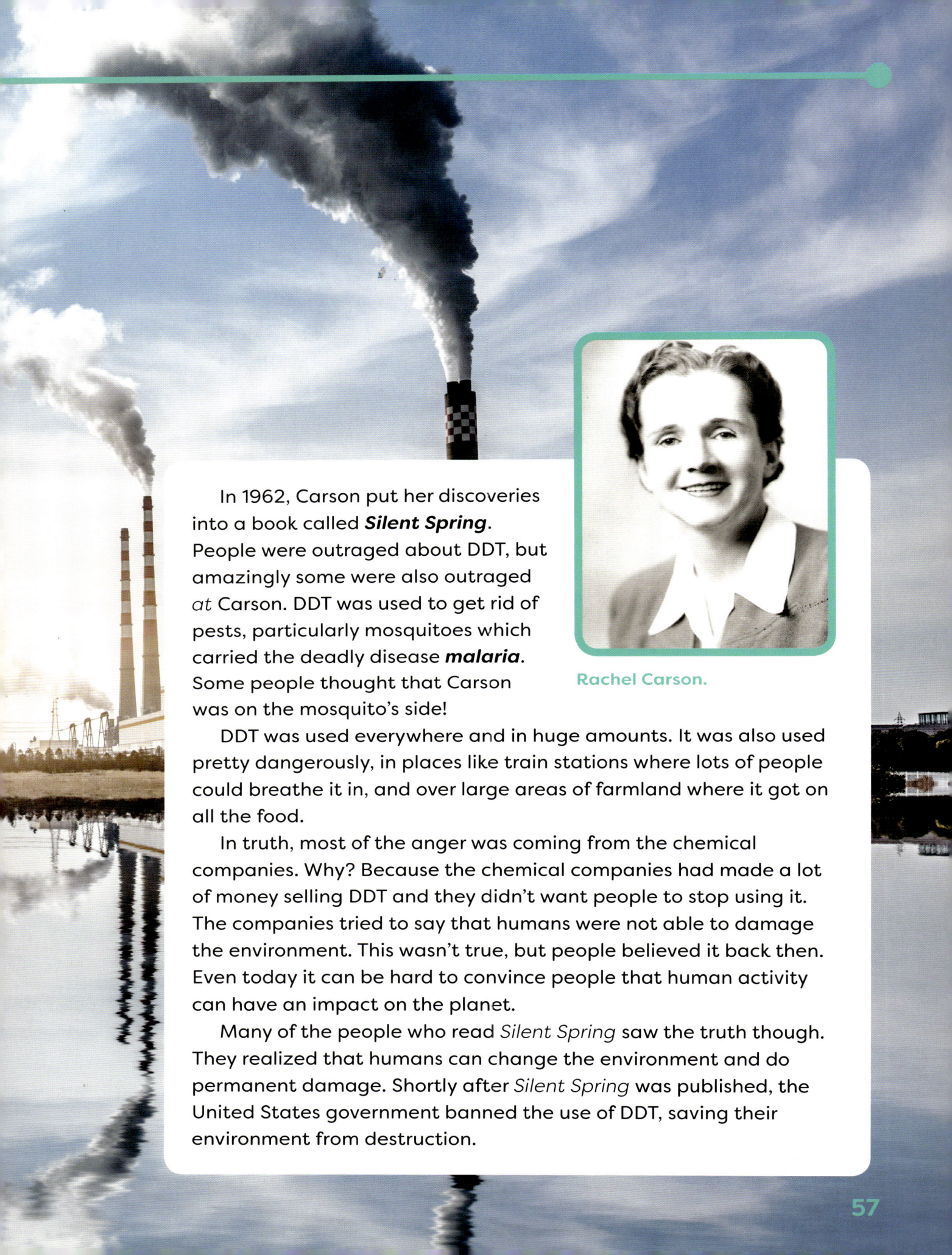

In 1962, Carson put her discoveries into a book called **Silent Spring**. People were outraged about DDT, but amazingly some were also outraged *at* Carson. DDT was used to get rid of pests, particularly mosquitoes which carried the deadly disease **malaria**. Some people thought that Carson was on the mosquito's side!

Rachel Carson.

DDT was used everywhere and in huge amounts. It was also used pretty dangerously, in places like train stations where lots of people could breathe it in, and over large areas of farmland where it got on all the food.

In truth, most of the anger was coming from the chemical companies. Why? Because the chemical companies had made a lot of money selling DDT and they didn't want people to stop using it. The companies tried to say that humans were not able to damage the environment. This wasn't true, but people believed it back then. Even today it can be hard to convince people that human activity can have an impact on the planet.

Many of the people who read *Silent Spring* saw the truth though. They realized that humans can change the environment and do permanent damage. Shortly after *Silent Spring* was published, the United States government banned the use of DDT, saving their environment from destruction.

HUMANS CHANGING THE ENVIRONMENT

Humans seem pretty small compared to the Earth. But can humans change the environment? Many scientists have shown that we can, and that we need to be careful. If not, we might damage the environment forever, and without the environment we won't survive.

Rachel Carson

Olga Owens Huckins woke up one morning to a strange sound. Or really, to no sound at all. Because all the birds on her land had died. She believed a chemical called **DDT** (short for **Dichlorodiphenyltrichloroethane**) was slowly poisoning the environment and she wrote to her friend, the famous American biologist and author, Rachel Carson. Carson did her own research and agreed that DDT was having a terrible effect. Plants, animals and even humans were experiencing the negative effects of the chemicals. It was making everyone sick.

INTERESTING FACT: One of the things that really inspired people to finally stop using DDT was the evidence that it was killing rare bald eagles. Actually, the DDT was getting into the eagle's eggs and making them too soft to carry chicks. Bald eagles are the national bird of the United States and Americans are very proud of them. The possibility that their favorite bird might actually be killed by their own actions was enough to push them into making changes.

The History of the Whole Universe

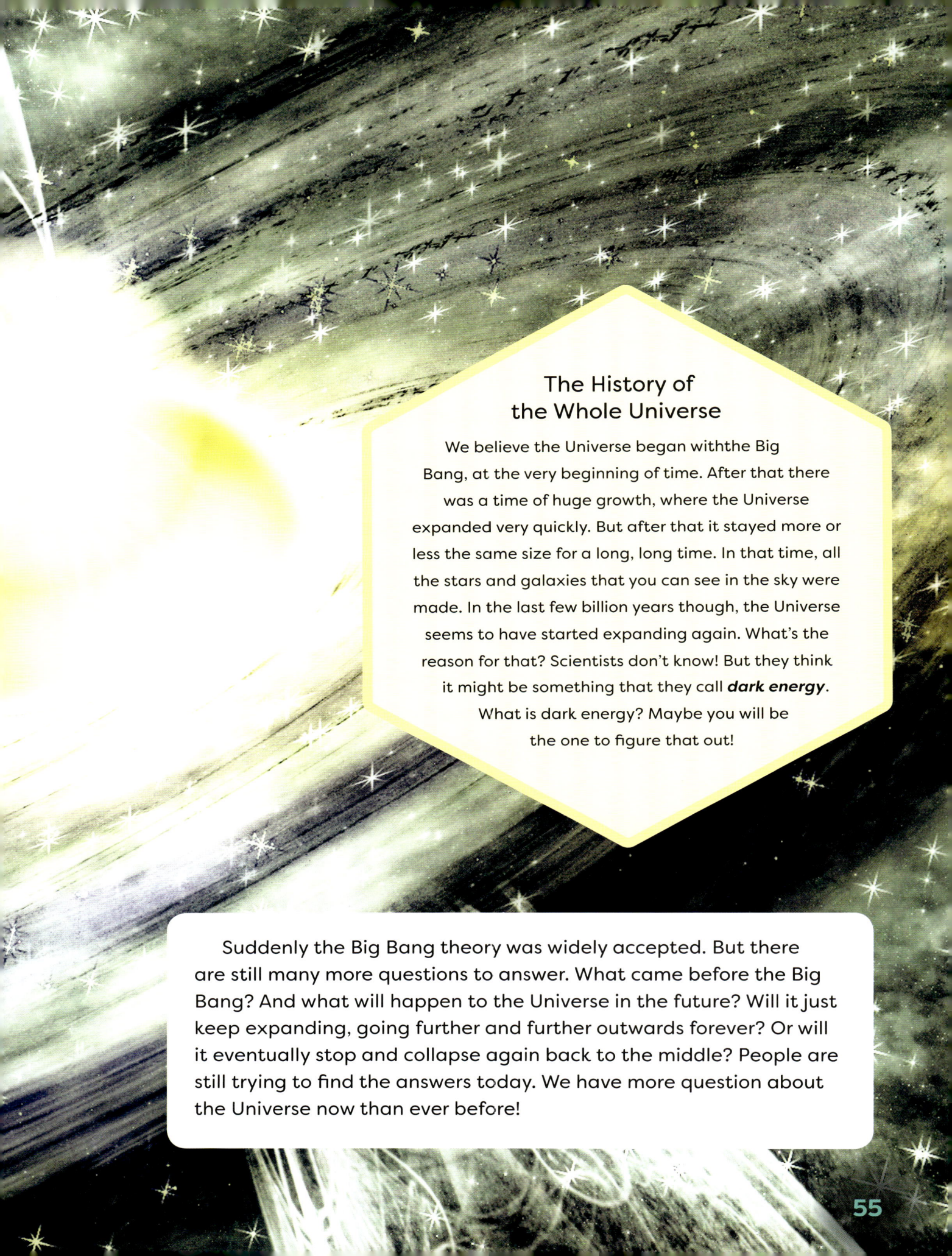

We believe the Universe began with the Big Bang, at the very beginning of time. After that there was a time of huge growth, where the Universe expanded very quickly. But after that it stayed more or less the same size for a long, long time. In that time, all the stars and galaxies that you can see in the sky were made. In the last few billion years though, the Universe seems to have started expanding again. What's the reason for that? Scientists don't know! But they think it might be something that they call **dark energy**. What is dark energy? Maybe you will be the one to figure that out!

Suddenly the Big Bang theory was widely accepted. But there are still many more questions to answer. What came before the Big Bang? And what will happen to the Universe in the future? Will it just keep expanding, going further and further outwards forever? Or will it eventually stop and collapse again back to the middle? People are still trying to find the answers today. We have more question about the Universe now than ever before!

Arno Penzias and Robert Wilson

Eventually, some other scientists agreed that the Big Bang must have happened like Lemaitre said. Many other scientists wanted to see proof. But if it happened 13.7 billion years ago, where could they find the evidence?

In the 1960s two American scientists named Arno Penzias and Robert Wilson were testing a new radar designed to detect **microwaves**. Microwaves are not just for cooking food. They are a kind of light that we can't see with our eyes. Almost by accident, Penzias and Wilson found that there were a lot of microwaves coming from all around. A lot more than they were expecting. After doing some research, they realized that they had found something called the **cosmic microwave background**. Sounds fancy right? This background is the leftover light from the Big Bang! Some of the light from the Big Bang is still bouncing around, and this is what Penzias and Wilson found!

INTERESTING FACT: This picture (below) shows what the cosmic microwave background looks like when we turn the microwaves into colors we can see. Looks pretty messy, right? Well, that's because it's what's left of the biggest explosion ever! When you look at this picture, you are looking back in time to what is left from the very beginning of the Universe itself.

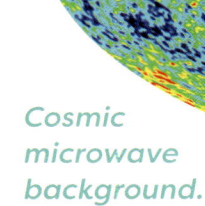

Cosmic microwave background.

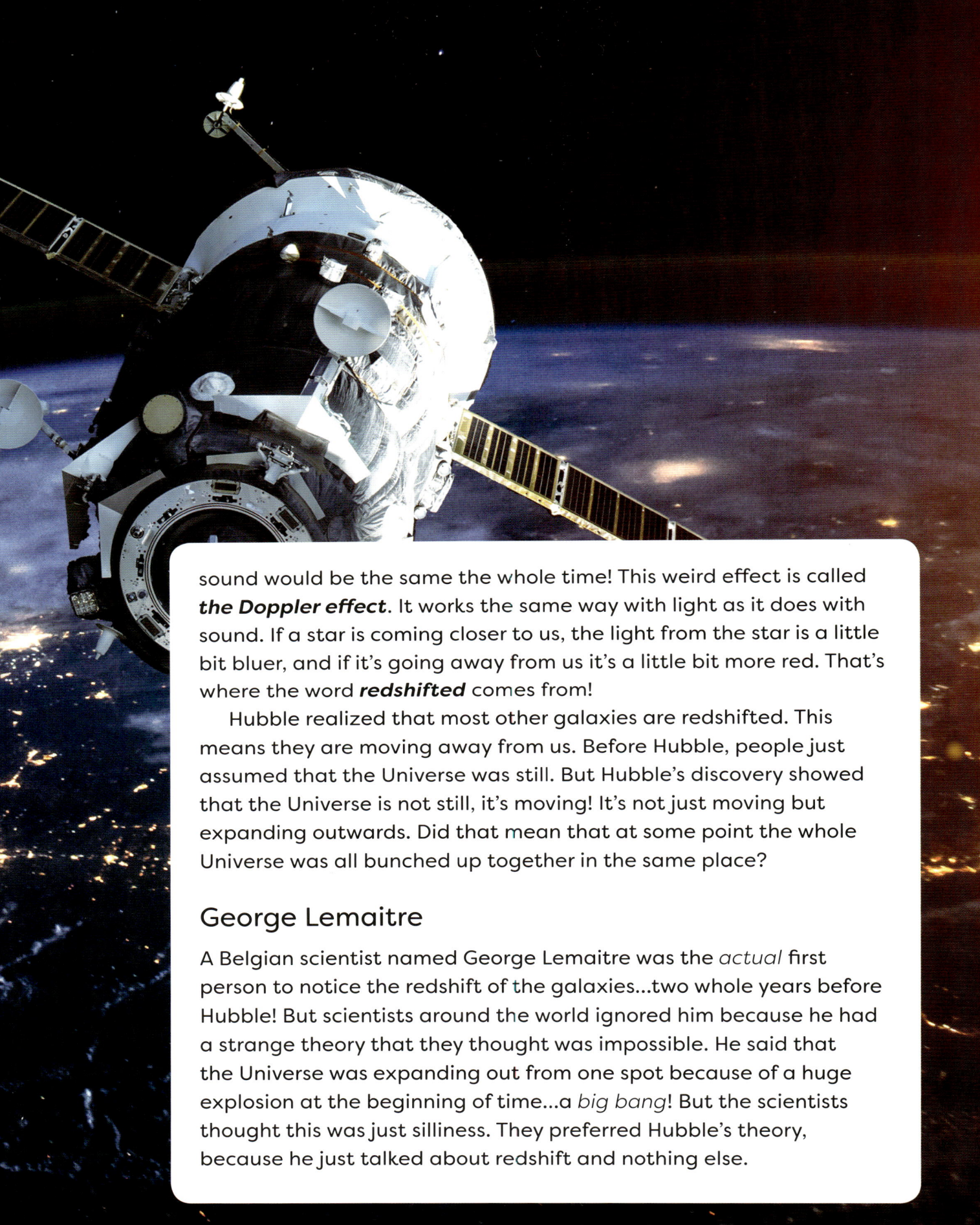

sound would be the same the whole time! This weird effect is called **the Doppler effect**. It works the same way with light as it does with sound. If a star is coming closer to us, the light from the star is a little bit bluer, and if it's going away from us it's a little bit more red. That's where the word **redshifted** comes from!

Hubble realized that most other galaxies are redshifted. This means they are moving away from us. Before Hubble, people just assumed that the Universe was still. But Hubble's discovery showed that the Universe is not still, it's moving! It's not just moving but expanding outwards. Did that mean that at some point the whole Universe was all bunched up together in the same place?

George Lemaitre

A Belgian scientist named George Lemaitre was the *actual* first person to notice the redshift of the galaxies...two whole years before Hubble! But scientists around the world ignored him because he had a strange theory that they thought was impossible. He said that the Universe was expanding out from one spot because of a huge explosion at the beginning of time...a *big bang*! But the scientists thought this was just silliness. They preferred Hubble's theory, because he just talked about redshift and nothing else.

The Andromeda galaxy.

INTERESTING FACT: The Andromeda galaxy is our nearest *intergalactic* neighbor. The Universe is a pretty big place. Our own Sun is just one star in the Milky Way galaxy, which has more than 100 billion other stars! The Milky Way is part of something bigger called the **Local Group**. The Local Group has more than 54 galaxies in it. But it is just a part of something even bigger called the **Virgo Supercluster**. And there are more than 10 million *other* superclusters in the Universe... that we can see! There might be even more out there that are so far away that the light from them hasn't reached us yet!

INTERESTING FACT: In honor of his discovery, the **Hubble Space Telescope** was named after Edwin Hubble. It orbits in space around the Earth, more than 500 km above the surface. It may seem strange to put a telescope in space, but a space telescope can get pictures a lot clearer than on Earth. In fact, the Hubble telescope has taken some of the best pictures we've ever seen of faraway places in the Universe. It's also been an important part in proving many aspects of the Big Bang theory. It collects a huge amount of data for scientists to use.

The Hubble Space Telescope.

But what is **redshift**? Well, the same effect that causes redshift also changes the sound of cars as they drive past you. Have you ever listened to a car drive past you really fast? As it comes towards you, it makes a *yeeee* sort of noise. But when it has gone past, the sound changes to a *yooow* sort of noise. But if you were in that car, the

from photographs. She had to look at photographs because women weren't allowed to use the telescope!

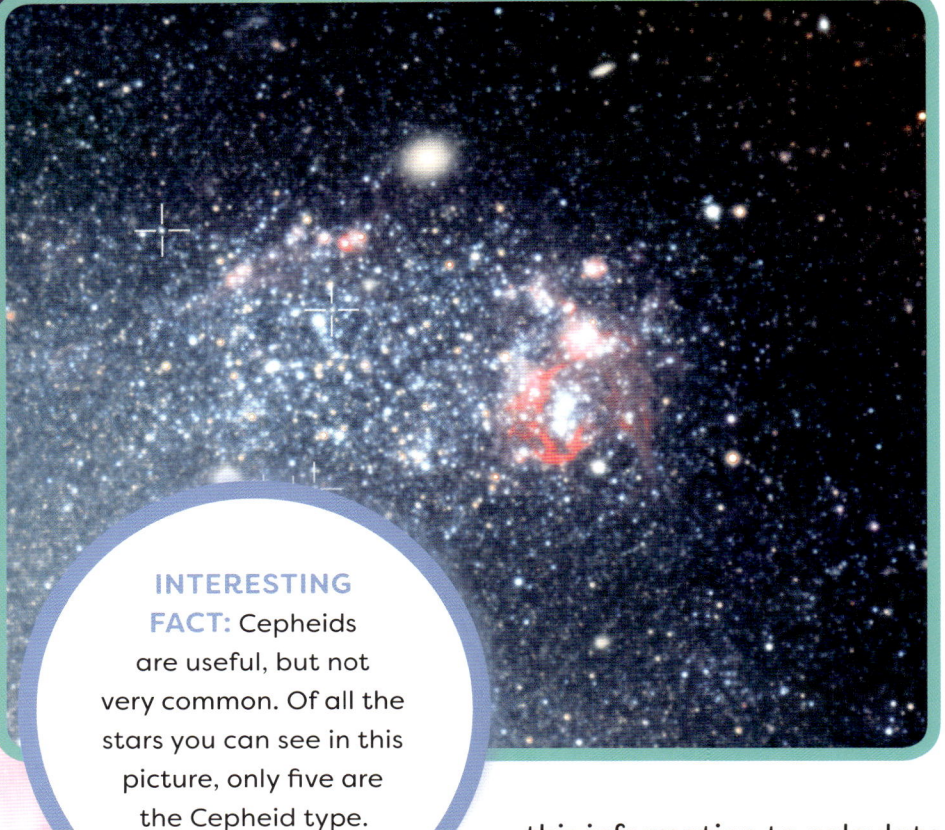

She noticed that certain stars, called **Cepheids**, changed brightness in different photos. They were actually flashing. She realized that the length of the flashes was always connected to the brightness of the star. She used this information to calculate the distance to the star. After many years of fighting for her ideas to be published, she finally won. Today, we call the rule about brightness and distance **Leavitt's Law**. And she did it all even though she was partially deaf for most of her life!

INTERESTING FACT: Cepheids are useful, but not very common. Of all the stars you can see in this picture, only five are the Cepheid type.

Edwin Hubble

In the 1920s, American astronomer Edwin Hubble was looking at **nebulas**, which are huge clouds that eventually turn into stars. Using **Leavitt's Law**, Hubble realized that some of these nebulas were much further away than anybody realized. He had discovered that some of these clouds were not nebulas at all but were **other galaxies**. These galaxies were filled with millions and billions of their own stars. The closest major galaxy, called Andromeda, is about **24,000,000,000,000,000,000 kilometers** away! Nobody thought distances like that were even possible. Everyone thought that all the stars in the Universe were in our galaxy, which is called **the Milky Way**. Hubble kept looking for new galaxies and eventually realized something strange. They were all **redshifted**.

THE BIG BANG THEORY

How big is the Universe? How old? And how did it begin?

All these questions are answered by **the Big Bang theory**. The Big Bang theory is all about the start of the universe itself. It looks towards the farthest and oldest p laces in the universe, the very edge of what we know. It asks some of the most important questions about how everything around us came to be.

Henrietta Swann Leavitt

People are fascinated by questions like 'How big is the universe?' But how do you measure something as far away as a star? The very closest star to Earth (aside from the Sun) is **Proxima Centauri**. That is more than **40,000,000,000,000 kilometers** away! Close stars can be measured using something called the **parallax effect**. If they are close enough, we can measure their movement and compare it to the movement of the Earth. But nobody could figure out how to measure the distance of the far away stars.

INTERESTING FACT: The above is a photo of a room full of **computers** at Harvard University. You can see Leavitt standing in the middle. In the front of the room, looking through a viewing machine, you can see another famous scientist named Annie Jump Cannon. She invented the system we use to categorize different types of stars! For example, our Sun is a **G2V type star**. Just like Leavitt, Cannon was also not allowed to look through any telescopes and was also partially deaf!

Henrietta Swann Leavitt worked in the 1890s as a **computer**. The male professors called the women who worked at Harvard University in the United States computers – people who did jobs like **computing** the numbers in complicated equations. Computers did the math and other work that the professors didn't want to do themselves. Henrietta's job was to record the brightness of stars into energy you would make almost **90,000,000,000,000,000 joules of energy**! That's more energy than is made by 20,000 tons of dynamite. That weighs the same as 3,500 African elephants!

Scientists and politicians soon realized that if they could control this energy, it would make a powerful weapon. During the Second World War, a race began to make this weapon. The secret name for the project in the United States of America was **the Manhattan Project**. This was led by a physicist named Robert Oppenheimer. The American scientists realized that one type of uranium was very easy to split apart. When it split apart, it released *a lot* of energy. The energy from one atom splitting then made other atoms split too. This went on and on, releasing all the energy at once. This is called a **chain reaction** and was how the first atomic bomb worked. Only one *fiftieth* of the uranium in the first ever atomic bomb turned into energy, but it was still enough to destroy an entire city.

Atomic bombs were only ever used two times in war. They were dropped on the Japanese cities of **Hiroshima** and **Nagasaki**. Hundreds of thousands of people died in the initial explosion. Millions more died from the poisonous effects of the radioactivity, just like Marie Curie.

Fortunately, since then no more bombs have been used in war. But the most powerful countries in the world still keep making bigger and more powerful bombs even today. Now they have bombs which use hydrogen rather than uranium. These **hydrogen** bombs are a thousand times more powerful than the uranium bombs and make explosions hotter than the surface of the Sun.

These bombs have changed the world completely. Now humans have the weapons to completely wipe themselves out. The important lesson here is that science is not good or bad, but people can use science to do both amazing and terrible things. It's the choices that we make that are good or bad, not the science.

INTERESTING FACT: Ever wondered what keeps the Sun burning so hot? It's actually the same type of nuclear reaction as in a hydrogen bomb! All stars, including the Sun, are just big hydrogen bombs that have been exploding for billions of years. Our Sun is about 4.6 billion years old and has been exploding constantly for that whole time. It will probably keep exploding for billions and billions of years.

For example, oxygen has eight protons, iron has twenty-six protons, uranium has ninety-two protons, and just a single proton all by itself is hydrogen. Rutherford discovered that when atoms shoot off radioactive particles, these are sometimes protons. *But* if the number of protons changes then the type of atom must change as well! That's how uranium turns into lead!

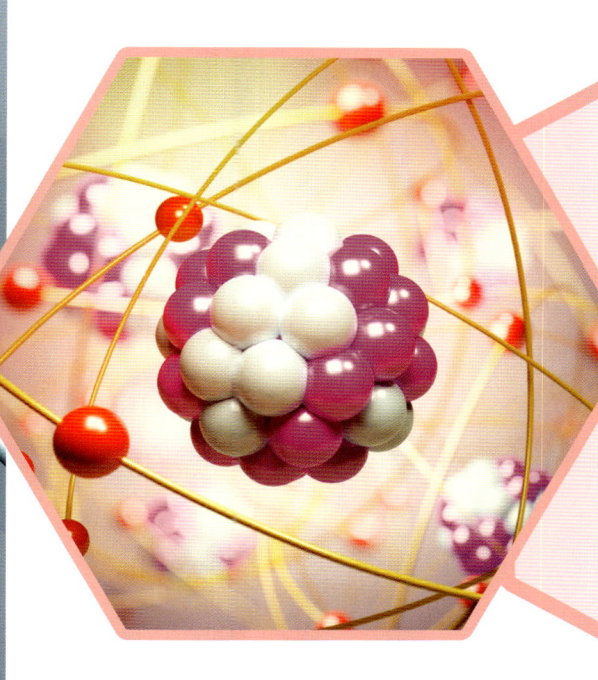

Atomic Models

Rutherford's model had only two parts - the nucleus in the middle and the electrons flying around the outside. Now we know that the nucleus has both protons and neutrons. But even more weird is that now we don't think of the electron orbiting the nucleus like the Moon around the Earth. Instead, electrons move so fast that they make a **cloud** and the electron could actually be anywhere in that cloud at any time! The world of atoms is a weird and wonderful place and it gets weirder all the time.

Manhattan Project

So scientists figured out how radioactive particles came out of the nucleus of the atom. But what about that strange and powerful energy? Albert Einstein had already figured out the secret of the energy in 1905. He said that **matter** and **energy** were two types of the same thing. One could *become* the other. The amount of energy made could be calculated using the famous equation, **$E=mc^2$**. This equation means that:

The energy produced by some matter **EQUALS** its weight **MULTIPLIED** by the speed of light and then ***MULTIPLIED by the speed of light again***!

The speed of light is already a huge number, but if you multiply it by itself, it's ridiculously big. If you turned 1 gram of atoms completely

Types of Radioactivity

There are actually three main types of radiation. **Radiation** is the name for anything that comes out of an atom because of radioactivity. The first two types of radiation are tiny particles. **Alpha** particles are the first type in this picture. They are made of two protons and two neutrons all joined together. For radiation, Alpha particles are actually quite big. They are not able to even go through something as thin as a piece of paper.

Beta particles are the second type in this picture. These are actually just a single electron. These electrons are different to all the other electrons that are in an atom, because they come out of the middle part of the atom (the **nucleus**), not the outside part where the electrons normally are. Beta particles are much smaller than Alpha particles but can still be stopped by an aluminum sheet.

The last type of radiation is not made of particles, but energy. These are called **Gamma** rays. They are a kind of light wave but with so much energy that they can damage other atoms. You can need up to 13 feet (4 meters) of lead to stop these dangerous rays of light.

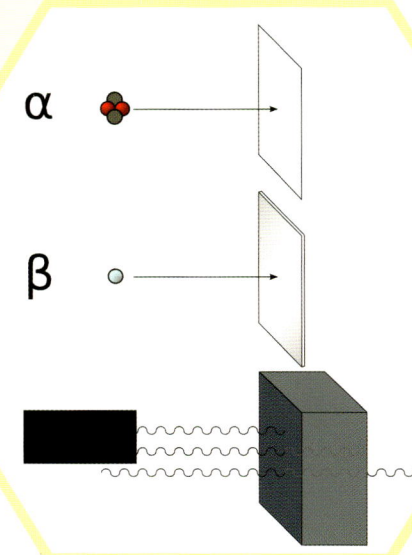

Ernest Rutherford

Ernest Rutheford.

A New Zealand scientist named Ernest Rutherford also did experiments with radioactivity at around the same time as Curie. He discovered that *most of the time* when you shoot radioactive particles at very thin gold foil they go straight through...but *sometimes* they bounce back!

After careful testing, Rutherford realized that atoms must be mostly just empty space. Rutherford realized that the **electrons** which made electricity flew around a tiny bit of matter in the middle of the atom, which he called the **nucleus**. In the nucleus are particles called **protons**. The number of these protons decide what kind of element the atom is.

SPLITTING THE ATOM

Imagine you have a rock. Now split it in half. And then take one of the halves and split it again. Keep doing that, again and again and again. What would happen? Do you think that you could keep splitting it into smaller and smaller pieces forever? Or would you eventually get something that can't be split apart? For a long time, scientists thought that the atom was as small as you could go. No one could break it apart into anything smaller. But when scientists did eventually split the atom apart, they discovered incredible and terrifying power.

Marie Curie

In 1896, a scientist named Henri Becquerel noticed something strange about the element called uranium. It randomly shoots out **particles** and a **powerful kind of energy**. Stranger than that, the uranium also slowly transformed into lead. For hundreds of years people had thought that was impossible!

The Polish scientist Marie Curie was one of the first people to look into this strange new energy. She called it **radioactivity**. She made huge discoveries about what it was and how it worked. Using radioactivity, she discovered two new elements, **radium** and **polonium**. Unfortunately, nobody knew how dangerous radioactivity was. Curie eventually died from an illness caused by the effect of radioactivity. Even today, if you look at her original notes you have to wear a special suit to protect yourself from the radioactive particles still on them.

In 1932, another physicist named James Chadwick discovered another part of the atom called the **neutron**. Neutrons holds the nucleus together. Finally, scientists had figured out the major parts of the atom.

Marie Curie.

INTERESTING FACT: Marie Curie is the only person to ever win two **Nobel Prizes** in different sciences, one in Physics in 1903 and one in Chemistry in 1911. She was also the first woman to ever receive a Nobel Prize!

Future Medicine

Even though vaccines and antibiotics have saved millions of lives, people today are still afraid of them. Some people think that vaccines are dangerous, even though almost all scientists say they are safe. Because of this, some people don't take vaccines, and so some diseases that were nearly wiped out are back again! Antibiotics are also in trouble. People misuse antibiotics all the time. This can make the bacteria even stronger than the drugs and create new **superbugs**! Everybody needs to understand how medicines work and how to use them to finally stop these diseases.

There are still many illnesses in the world today for which we have no cures. Maybe you will be the researcher who cures a disease, or a doctor who treats illnesses and teaches people about the importance of medicines!

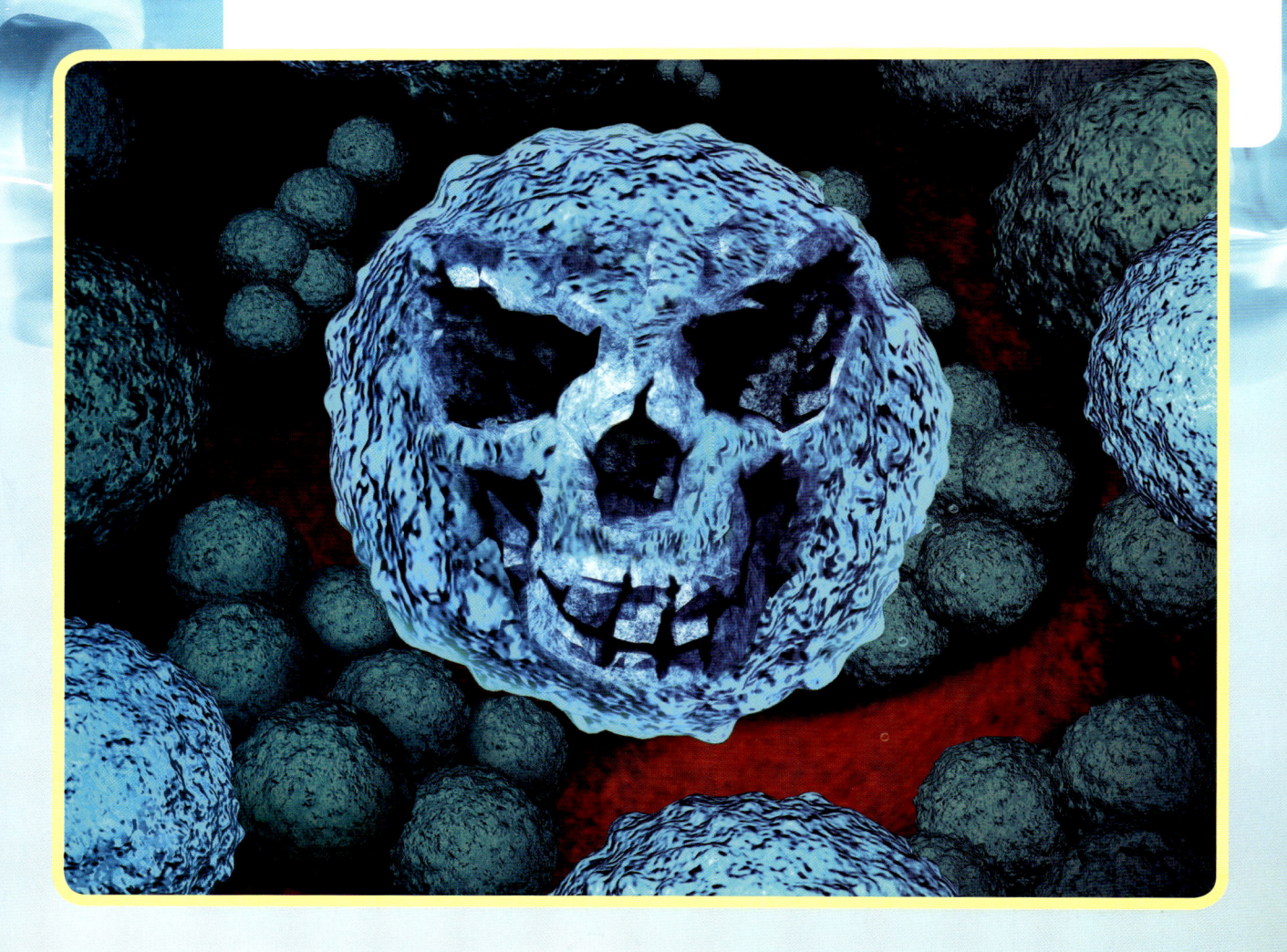

Penicillium conidiophores.

INTERESTING FACT: This is a picture of the part of the penicillium fungus called the *conidiophores*. This purpose of this part of the fungus is to send out *spores*. Spores are just like fungus seeds. They go out into the world and, if they land somewhere with food and water, they can start a new fungus.

Alexander Fleming

People in the Twentieth Century invented more and more vaccines for stopping viruses. But there was still no treatment for bacteria. These still killed millions of people every year.

Sometimes, discoveries in science can happen purely by accident. In the 1920s, a Scottish doctor and scientist named Alexander Fleming was studying some bacteria. Even though he was very clever, his lab was usually very messy. While he was away on holiday some **penicillium** fungus accidentally grew and killed the bacteria he was studying. Fleming swapped to studying the fungus instead. He realized that the fungus could make a chemical that killed bacteria. Over the next twenty years, he and other scientists figured out how to make the chemical in a factory. Fleming called it **penicillin**. Today scientists have made dozens of different **antibiotic** drugs to kill different kinds of bacteria, but they all started with penicillin.

The Immune System

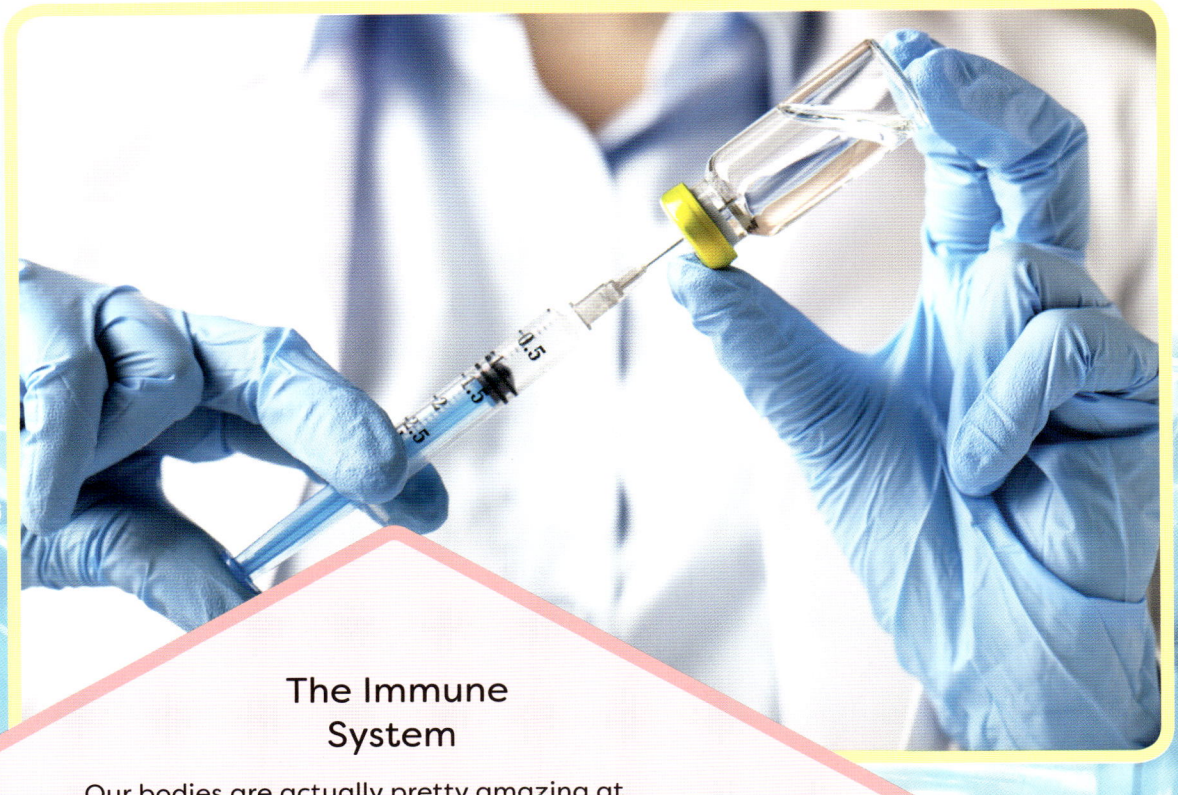

Our bodies are actually pretty amazing at defending themselves from harmful invaders like viruses and bacteria. We have something called an *immune system*. The immune system is made up of millions of cells and chemicals in your body which stop deadly diseases.

Unfortunately, sometimes people's immune systems aren't strong enough to fight back, or the disease spreads too fast for the immune system to learn how to beat it. Vaccines work by giving the body a weak or dead version of the disease to practice on. That way when the real disease comes, the body knows how to deal with it! The yellow cell in this picture is a part of the immune system called a *neutrophil* or *white blood cell*. The orange cell is a *bacterium* called *anthrax*. As you can see, the white blood cell is attacking and destroying the anthrax.

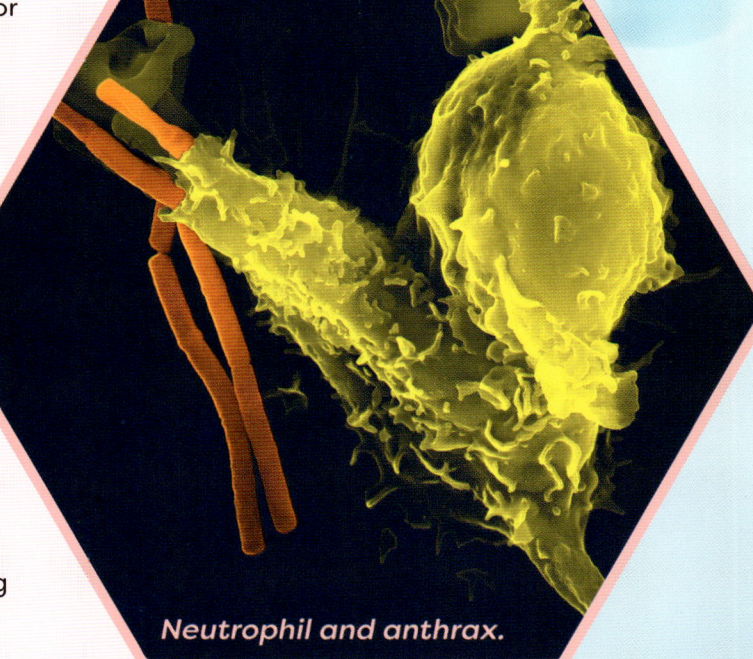

Neutrophil and anthrax.

Louis Pasteur

People knew about the existence of **microorganisms** like bacteria for more than a hundred years before John Snow's time, but nobody really knew what they were, where they came from or how they worked. They didn't think there were very many of them and had no reason to think they caused disease.

A French chemist named Louis Pasteur changed all of that. Between the 1840s and the 1890s, Pasteur made many discoveries about both chemistry and biology. Before Pasteur, people thought microorganisms, and even small creatures like fleas, were created randomly from dust and particles. They called this **spontaneous generation**. Pasteur proved that they were dead wrong. He showed if you boiled a liquid in a closed container then no microorganisms grew. The microorganisms must come from outside and then multiply. This proved **germ theory**!

People today still remove bacteria from liquids like milk, wine and beer using a method Pasteur invented, called **pasteurization**. It was another step towards stopping people from getting sick from the bacteria in their food and drink. Louis Pasteur also created new vaccines for diseases like anthrax and rabies and did a lot to figure out how vaccines work. His understanding of tiny living things led to huge improvements in understanding how disease spreads. It's because of him that doctors wash their hands!

Louis Pasteur working in his laboratory.

John Snow

In the 1800s there was a terrible disease in London, England, called **cholera**. Cholera still kills people around the world today. By 1854, it had killed more than ten thousand people. London in 1854 had more than two million people but *no sewers*! The city was absolutely disgusting. All the sewage and rubbish went into the main river, called the Thames. The scientists at the time thought that the smell coming off the Thames must be causing cholera. They called it **miasma**, but there was no proof this was the cause of the disease. Even though people covered their faces and stayed indoors, nothing seemed to stop cholera from spreading.

A doctor named John Snow decided to find his own answers. He very carefully tracked all the people who became sick. After months of looking at his records, he realized that the sick people were all getting water from the same water pump. They shut down the pump and people stopped getting sick! Snow tried to tell people that this was proof that there was something in the water spreading from person to person. This idea was called **germ theory**. But Snow was mostly ignored by the scientists.

> **INTERESTING FACT:** John Snow was already famous for inventing **anesthesia**, which is the kind of drug used to knock people out. Before that, people would have surgery while they were *still awake*!

> **INTERESTING FACT:** John Snow realized that the **Broad Street pump** was the source of the deadly, disease carrying water. Today, this pump stands in the same place to remind us of the importance of John Snow's discovery.

VACCINES AND ANTIBIOTICS

Can you imagine what it would be like to live in a world where the flu might actually kill you? Or a cold? Or a cut on your arm? That is what the world was like, only a hundred years ago. Today you can go to the doctor, get a couple of medicines and, in a few days, you'll be all better. But it took thousands of years of science and research to get those pills into that bottle.

INTERESTING FACT: Viruses are so tiny that they can be very difficult to see. They are smaller than any other kind of living thing. They are so small that scientists aren't even sure if they count as being alive. They are really just a bunch of big, complicated molecules. But don't be fooled. They may be small, but viruses are some of the deadliest diseases in the world.

Edward Jenner

Smallpox is one of the deadliest diseases ever known. In the last 100 years, smallpox killed more than 300 million people. Who knows how many people it's killed in the last ten thousand years? But thanks to a man named Edward Jenner, there is almost no smallpox left anywhere in the world.

Smallpox virus as seen through a microscope.

Edward Jenner realized that people who caught cowpox didn't catch smallpox. Cowpox was a disease like smallpox but much milder and usually not deadly. After some experimentation, in 1796 Jenner made the first ***vaccine***. He infected people with the mildest type of cowpox so they didn't get smallpox. It was an incredible discovery that saved countless lives, but it took 181 years to stop the disease once and for all. Still, Jenner did not really understand *how* his vaccines worked.

Species Adapt To Their Environments

In fact, both of the elephants alive today were once the same species but grew apart as they *adapted* to suit their environments. How and why are these elephants different? Asian elephants are smaller so that they can move around between trees in Asian jungles. Meanwhile African elephants are bigger, partly so that they can protect themselves from the fearsome African hunting animals like lions and leopards.

Biologists often use tree diagrams like this to show how animals are related to one another. This tree diagram from 1868 was drawn by a biologist called Ernst Haeckel. As you can see, he put all the names of the different living things known at the time on an actual tree to show people how they related to one another. Of course, he put humans or 'Man' at the very top. But are humans really that important?

Compare that tree to this other, more modern tree diagram. Where are humans on this one? We are just one of millions of different species that are all part of the one tiny branch that says 'animals'. Can you find that branch in amongst all the other weird and wonderful names? And every plant in the world is all on the one tiny branch that says plants. Scientists today now know about so many different kinds of living things that compared to all of them, humans just aren't important enough to get a space on the tree. In fact, almost all of the types of living thing that you can see on this tree are too small to see with the naked eye.

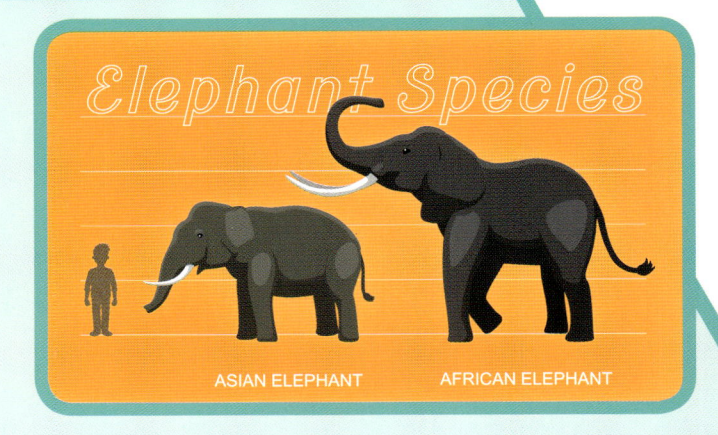

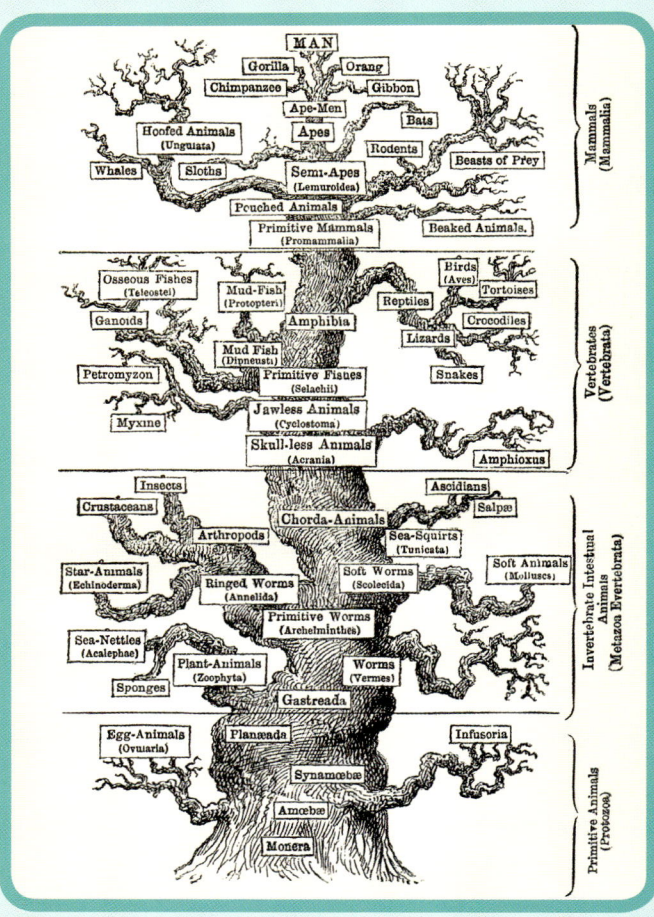

Elephant Species

ASIAN ELEPHANT   AFRICAN ELEPHANT

Haeckel's tree of life.

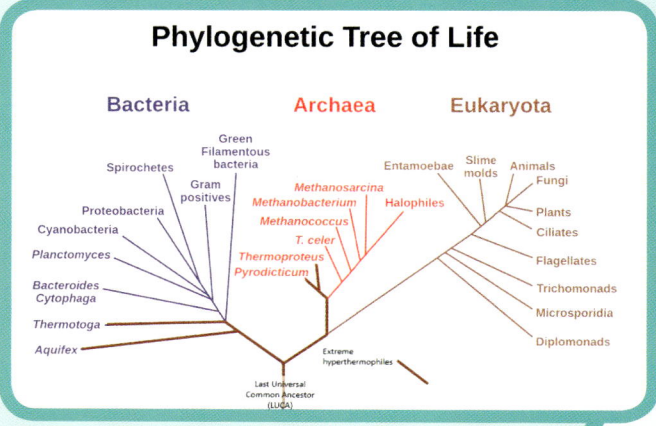

Modern tree diagram.

Scientists have split the timeline of the Earth into a lot of different chunks. The biggest chunks are called eons. The eons are then split into pieces called eras. The eras are then split into pieces called periods, and then the periods into epochs and then the epochs into ages.

Humans have only been around for the very last age of the very last epoch of the very last period of the very last era of the very last eon (what a mouthful!). The closer to now, the more we know, but the further back you go, the less and less we know. The constantly changing surface of the Earth destroys the evidence that we need to see back in time to the beginning of our planet. But our science is also getting better and better all the time!

Darwin saw that all living things change very, very slowly over time. By understanding this, we can see where all the different living things come from. Billions of years ago, the very first ever living thing had children. Then its children had children and so on and on. Eventually those children became the huge variety of things that have ever lived. We are the children of that tiny living thing. So is every mammal, fish, insect, bird, tree, bush and fungus. So is every living thing that we can see all around us. Every living thing is related. We are all part of the same family and we are all evolving and changing, very slowly over millions of years.

other animals and plants he saw all around the world, from tropical islands to the Amazon rainforest to hot, dry deserts. He saw how all living things, even people, were connected. He called his theory the ***Theory of Evolution***. This is how it works.

Imagine some African elephants. They love hot weather. But what if the weather gets cooler? What if an ice age came slowly over tens of thousands of years? Elephants have a little bit of hair to protect them, but some have more hair than others. The ones with more hair are protected from the cold, even just a little bit, and so are stronger and have more children than the ones without hair, and these children have even more hair than their parents. What happens next? More elephants now have more hair. Then the new elephants with more hair also have more children and the elephants with not very much hair have even fewer children. Slowly but surely, the hairier elephants have more children, and all the elephants become more hairy. Finally, after thousands and millions of years, they aren't elephants anymore...they are mammoths! This is how a new species of animals is created.

INTERESTING FACT: Mammoths are a type of elephant that lived during the most recent Ice Age, so they needed lots of woolly hair to survive in the cold weather. When the planet started heating up they died out and became extinct.

INTERESTING FACT: African elephants live in a warmer environment so they evolved to have less hair.

THE THEORY OF EVOLUTION

There are billions and billions of different **species** (or types) of living things on Earth. But how did they all come to be? Scientists tried to figure out the answer over thousands of years.

Aristotle

Aristotle was an ancient Greek philosopher who tried his hand at many sciences. He was one of the first people to start grouping animals together and looking for similarities. Aristotle thought that all the animals and plants he could see were the *only ones that had ever lived*. But fossils show that there are all kinds of extinct plants and animals, like mammoths and dinosaurs, that lived long ago. Some things living today have only been around recently. Where did they come from?

INTERESTING FACT: Aristotle's teacher was a very famous philosopher named Plato. And Plato had a very famous teacher named Socrates (you might remember these Ancient scientists from other chapters of this book). But Aristotle's student was probably the most famous of all of them – Alexander the Great! Alexander the Great was the king of a country named Macedonia and he went on to defeat the massive Persian Empire almost without losing a single battle. The empire Alexander made was one of the biggest ever and stretched all the way from Greece to India! But could he have done it without being taught by Aristotle?

Charles Darwin

Charles Darwin, an English biologist, cracked the mystery. In the 1830s he traveled around the world on a ship called the *Beagle*, all the way to the Galapagos Islands. The islands are so distant that the animals living there have been separated from the mainland for millions of years. It was the perfect place to study how animals grow and change. He also looked at

Charles Darwin.

INTERESTING FACT: Collecting fossils was dangerous work! Anning's whole family was in the fossil hunting business, and her father was seriously injured after falling from a cliff. But Mary Anning wasn't just a fossil hunter, she was a scientist. She spent a lot of time studying coprolites, even though she couldn't sell them, just to learn about dinosaurs. Not many tourists wanted to buy dinosaur poo!

Clair Cameron Patterson

People still didn't know how old the Earth actually was. Finally, in the 1960s, an American scientist named Clair Patterson turned his attention to the problem.

An interesting thing about radioactive elements is that as they release energy they *decay*. This means they change from bigger atoms into smaller ones. For example, one element called uranium turns slowly but surely into another element: lead. The scientists had figured out exactly how fast this happens. Patterson set out to measure the amount of lead in two different rocks. One had uranium in it and one didn't. If he could figure out how much uranium had turned into lead, he could figure out how old the rocks were, and therefore the age of the Earth!

Unfortunately, Patterson realized that his experiment was being *contaminated* by lead. It seemed to be everywhere! It was in the air, on his equipment, even in his skin and his hair. It was making his results all wrong. To get rid of the extra lead, he made the world's first *ultra-clean room*. This was a room so carefully cleaned and sealed that no extra lead could get into the experiment. Finally, he could calculate the age of the Earth: 4.55 billion years old.

There were many reasons why the discovery of the age of the Earth was so important. It made us see how small and young we are compared to our planet. If you imagined that a piece of paper represented the entire time that humans have been on Earth, then the whole history of the Earth would be a pile of paper more than three feet (one meter) tall. Humans would just be the one piece of paper on the very top!

INTERESTING FACT: After some investigation, Patterson realized that all the extra lead was actually caused by humans. For decades people had been putting lead into petrol to make their cars run better. This was a massive problem for humans and the environment as lead is a deadly poison! After spending years trying to get lead out of his laboratory, Patterson decided to try and get lead out of petrol too. He succeeded eventually, but it took more than 20 years of fighting chemical companies!

Mary Anning

In Mary Anning's time, people did not think you could achieve anything if you were poor or a woman. Anning was both, but she still became one of the most influential and important geologists ever. Mary discovered the complete skeletons of three different dinosaurs on English beaches in the early 1800s. Before this, only parts of skeletons had been found. She also explored the strange world of **coprolites**. These are dinosaur poo fossils! This may seem weird, but by looking at dinosaur poo Anning was able to discover more about dinosaurs than anyone before. She found out what they ate, what kinds of plants lived back then, and even how their bodies may have worked.

Anning's discoveries were hugely important. They showed that some animals lived long ago which don't exist anymore. This was a shocking surprise to people. Most people thought the only animals that ever lived were the ones they could see around them! Together Hutton and Anning made people see that the world was so much older than they realized.

INTERESTING FACT: Ever heard the rhyme 'she sells seashells by the sea shore?' That rhyme is about Mary Anning! No one in her time was willing to pay a poor woman to do science, so she survived by selling seashells to tourists, both real ones and fossils. She was even forced to sell all of her big fossil discoveries to pay her bills. I wonder how the rhyme would have gone if people had bought coprolites instead of seashells...

INTERESTING FACT: This picture is of a **plesiosaur** skeleton, like the ones that Anning found. Plesiosaurs are a kind of dinosaur that lived entirely in the sea, with four fins and a long thin neck. Can you imagine finding something like this if you didn't know what a dinosaur was? You might think you had found the bones of some sort of sea monster!

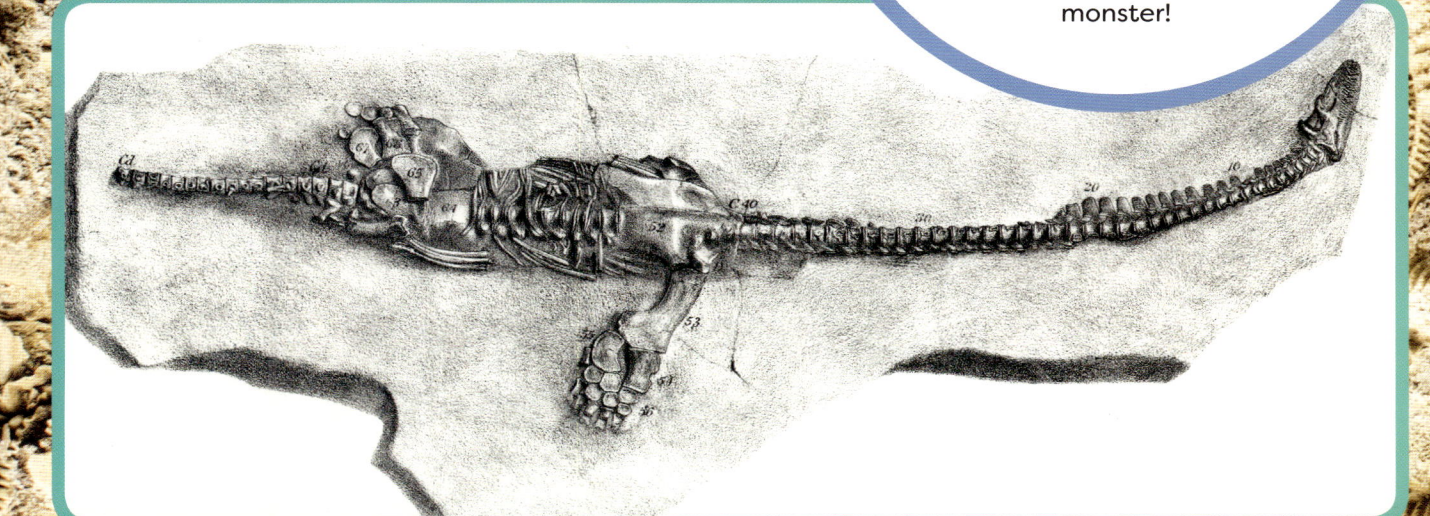

Geologists at the time had a big problem they could not solve. Why are there fossils of sea creatures on the top of mountains? How did they get there? One theory said that they must have been put there by a huge, global flood. But then where did all the water go afterwards?

Hutton came up with ideas to solve this and other problems. He suggested that the land wasn't fixed and unchanging, as people believed. It must sometimes be lifted up from underneath so that occasionally the bottom of the sea ends up at the top of mountains. He also suggested that the inside of the Earth must be hot enough for rocks to melt and flow like liquids. There are also currents there strong enough to change the Earth's surface. All these actions must take a long, *long* time to happen. Longer than anybody had previously thought possible. Millions and millions of years longer.

Unfortunately, Hutton's writing style was so bad that most people couldn't figure it out! During his lifetime he was almost completely unheard of. A friend rewrote his work after he died and people were finally able to understand his incredible work!

Hutton's Section

This famous bit of rock may not look too impressive, but it is an incredibly important formation. It's called **Hutton's Section**, named after James Hutton himself. Areas of exposed rock like this one and others around Edinburgh, where Hutton lived, were vital for giving him data and evidence to prove his theories. This is actually an area of rock that is newer and harder than the rock around it. It was lifted up by the incredible forces under the Earth's surface. While the rest of the softer rock around it was washed away, this harder rock was left behind.

THE AGE OF THE EARTH

If you ever walk through Jack Hills in Western Australia, you might get the feeling that the Earth is so old that it must have existed forever. The stones look so ancient that it feels like you are on another planet altogether. And in some ways, you are. Jack Hills has the oldest rocks in the world. They're called **hadean zircon** and are more than 4 *billion* years old. You can't find rocks like that anywhere else on Earth. The surface of the Earth is constantly changing and moving, so most of the rocks from that time are now gone. The study of the way that the Earth changes and what it's made of is called geology.

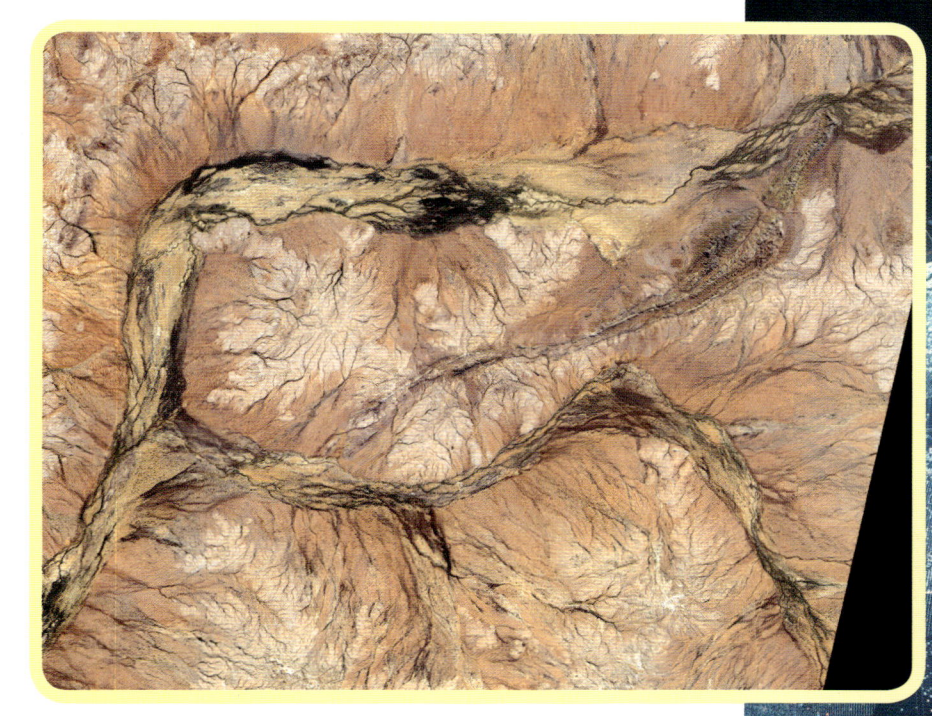

Jack Hills from above.

One of the most important questions for geologists, which took hundreds of years to answer, is very simple: how old is the Earth? The answer changed the way people thought about the Earth, and even the Universe as a whole.

James Hutton

Scottish scientist James Hutton is often called the **Father of Modern Geology**. He studied literature, law and chemistry, but in the 1750s he moved to his family farm. He used his scientific knowledge to improve the way that they farmed. He studied the land and the weather and soon started to realize things that nobody had before.

The Future

After that first flight, it only took 66 years for humans to walk on the Moon! The science of flight, also called **_aeronautics_**, is still making amazing discoveries today. Planes are going higher and faster than ever before and scientists and engineers are still finding ways to do more and more. When will we see the first flying car? Or a plane that can fly into space without a rocket? What about flying and landing a plane on Mars? These possibilities are all problems that are being solved right now! And tomorrow the world of flight will give us new problems we could never have imagined.

Orville and Wilbur Wright

The Wright brothers were a pair of American engineers. In 1903, they were the first to build something we might call an **aeroplane**. Their plane wasn't much more than a wooden glider with a small motor on it, but for its day it was the best technology around.

The Wright brothers showed us that sometimes you don't have to be really smart, just really hardworking. They designed and built their own wind tunnel, and then they tested over 200 wing designs to find the best one. Some of their first gliders didn't fly very well at all, but they kept working and never gave up. They built everything themselves, even the engine.

The first real flight only went about 120 feet (37 meters) – that's less than one Olympic swimming pool! But the people who saw it thought it was an incredible marvel. People were finally conquering gravity and taking to the air. Later the same day, the brothers managed to fly their machine 850 feet (260 meters)!

Orville Wright.

Wilbur Wright.

INTERESTING FACT: This is an incredible picture that shows the actual first ever powered flight made by humans. Given how rarely we are able to take pictures of the exact moment when great science happens, this photo is particularly special.

First flight.

George Cayley

Hot air balloons were invented in the late 1700s, but these were very large and impossible to steer. **Airships** which could be steered were invented in the 1850s. But these were huge, slow, and filled with explosive hydrogen gas!

Sir George Cayley was an English engineer. He was one of the first people to figure out some of the secrets of flying with wings. He worked in the early 1800s, long before the very first aeroplane. He studied the way that birds fly and how their wings worked. He tested his theories using experiments and discovered many of the most important lessons of flight like *air resistance* and *lift*. He did many demonstrations using gliders, showing how wings of different shapes and designs could make flights longer. But much like da Vinci before him, he did not have the technology to make a real aeroplane.

INTERESTING FACT: Hot air ballons were the earliest way people achieved flight – but they had some drawbacks, like no ability to steer!

FLIGHT

People today get into planes or helicopters without really thinking about how amazing flight is. But how did humans figure it out? How do you get hundreds of tons of metal to fly through the sky, floating on nothing but air?

Leonardo da Vinci

Leonardo da Vinci was a famous Italian artist that lived in the 1400s. He painted some of the most famous paintings in the world, like the *Mona Lisa*. But he also had an incredible mind for science and discovery. Among many other things, Da Vinci drew some incredible designs for flying machines. He never built them and he did not have the technology to make them work, but they were still way ahead of their time.

INTERESTING FACT: It was not easy to be a scientific person in medieval Europe. Any time people didn't understand something they called it 'witchcraft' and they did horrible things to 'witches'. Leonardo was so afraid of this, that his work was nearly all written in code. Unfortunately, by the time the codes were cracked, most of what he had worked out had been discovered by other people in the meantime!

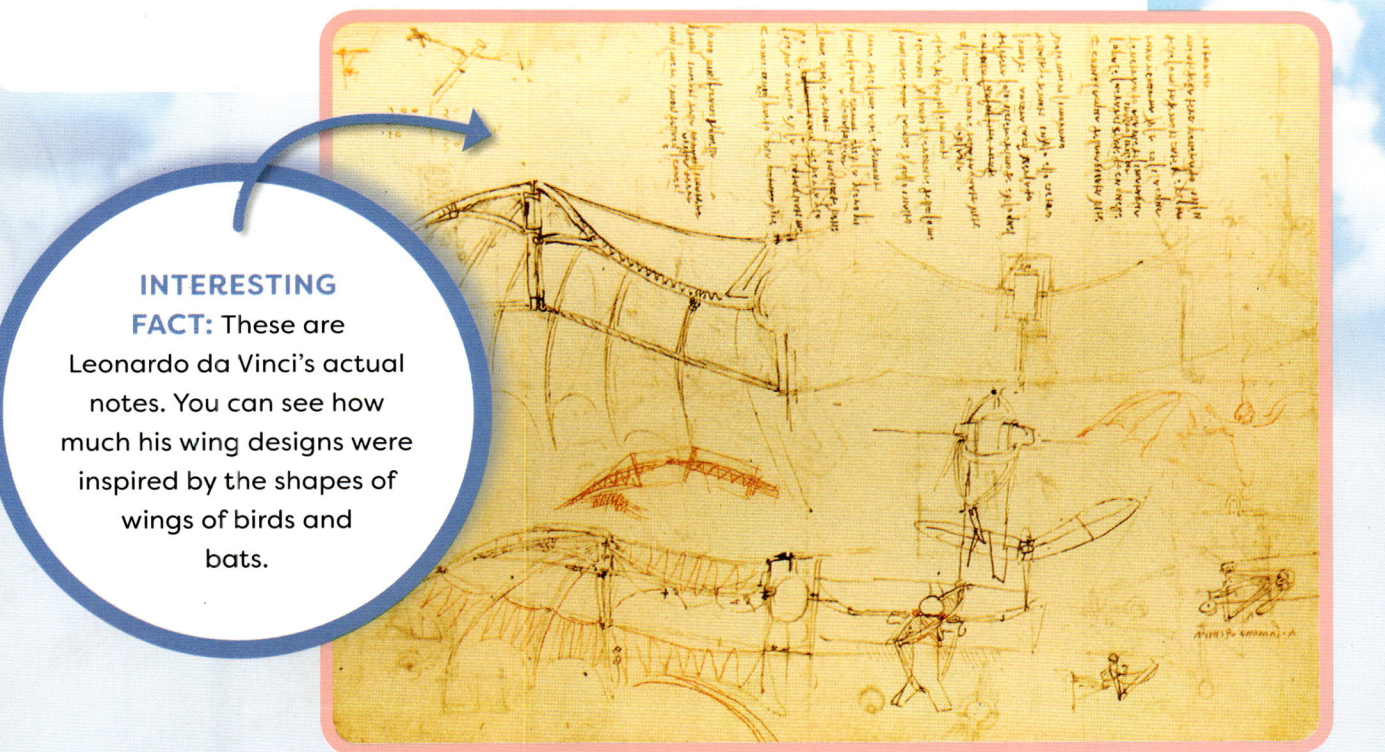

INTERESTING FACT: These are Leonardo da Vinci's actual notes. You can see how much his wing designs were inspired by the shapes of wings of birds and bats.

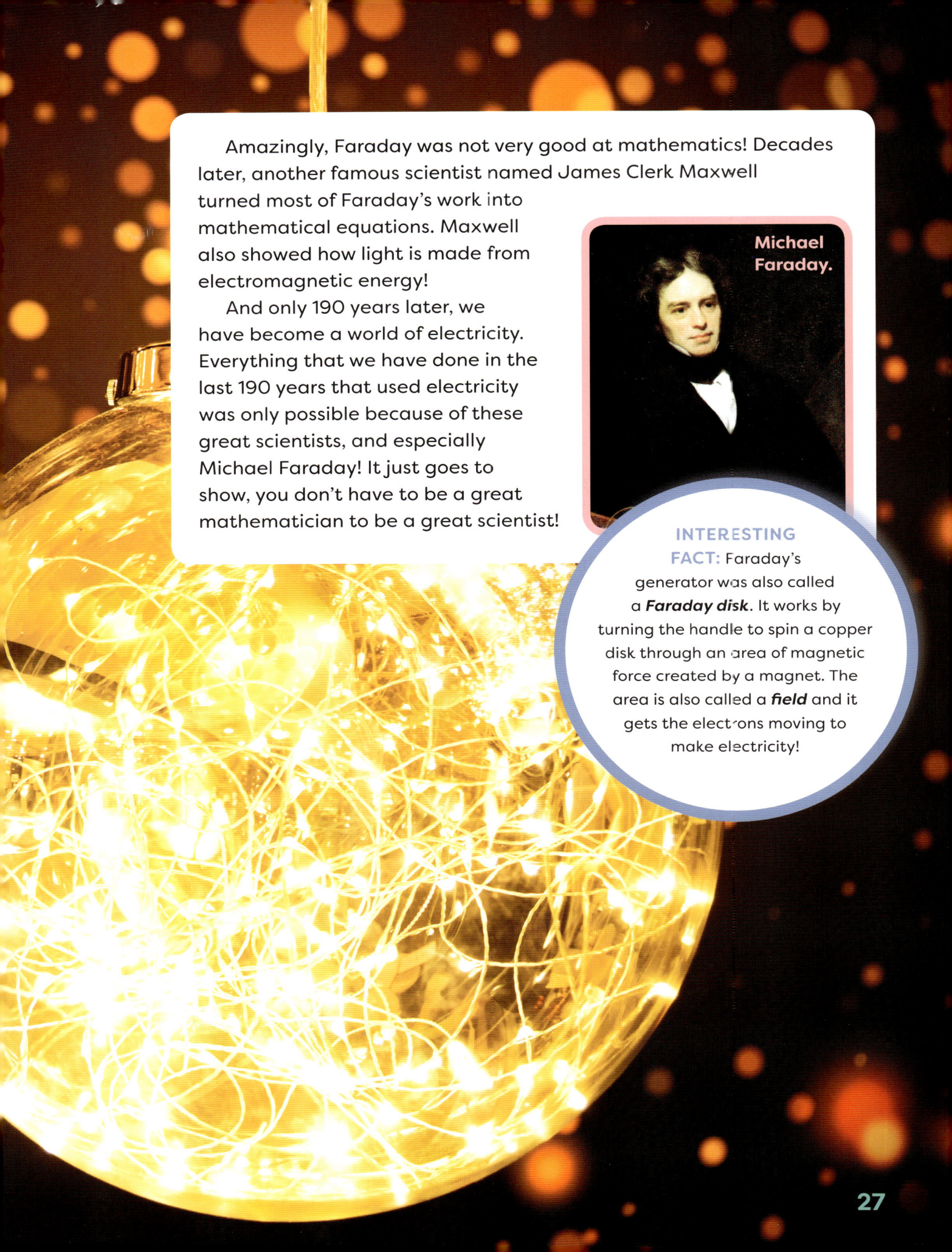

Amazingly, Faraday was not very good at mathematics! Decades later, another famous scientist named James Clerk Maxwell turned most of Faraday's work into mathematical equations. Maxwell also showed how light is made from electromagnetic energy!

And only 190 years later, we have become a world of electricity. Everything that we have done in the last 190 years that used electricity was only possible because of these great scientists, and especially Michael Faraday! It just goes to show, you don't have to be a great mathematician to be a great scientist!

Michael Faraday.

INTERESTING FACT: Faraday's generator was also called a **Faraday disk**. It works by turning the handle to spin a copper disk through an area of magnetic force created by a magnet. The area is also called a **field** and it gets the electrons moving to make electricity!

Michael Faraday

Now that people could make electricity with voltaic piles, scientists could work directly with electricity, and they started making incredible discoveries. No one did more important work than English scientist Michael Faraday. He discovered and wrote down the rules and laws that connected magnets and electricity, showing that they are two sides of the same force – *electromagnetism*.

Using this discovery, in 1831 he went on to invent a new machine, called a *generator,* which could also make electricity. Batteries are good at turning the energy of the different metals into electricity, but eventually they stop working when this *chemical energy* is used up. But Faraday's generator turned *movement* into electricity. Using a spinning disk, a magnet, a copper wire and his laws of *electromagnetism*, he was able to create much more electricity than ever before. Most of the electricity that is made today comes from generators which still use the same rules that Faraday discovered.

INTERESTING FACT: Today's generators, like this generator in the Hoover Dam in the United States, use the same laws as Faraday's. This generator is a *hydroelectric* generator. This means that it uses the power of moving water to spin big fans called *turbines*. They combine movement and a magnetic field to make enough electricity for millions of Americans!

Benjamin Franklin did a bit of everything, including helping to write the United States Constitution! In 1752, he conducted a famous experiment by flying a kite in a storm. Lightning struck the kite and Franklin captured it in something called a **Leyden jar**, which is used for storing electricity. This showed that electricity and lightning are the same thing!

Alessandro Volta

In 1800, Italian chemist Alessandro Volta invented something he called a **voltaic pile**. Basically, this is a stack of copper and zinc discs, and between each disc is a piece of paper soaked in salty water. When the top and the bottom of the stack are connected with copper wire, they made **flowing electricity**. Static electricity and capturing lightning were now a thing of the past. We still use voltaic piles every day, but now we call them **batteries**!

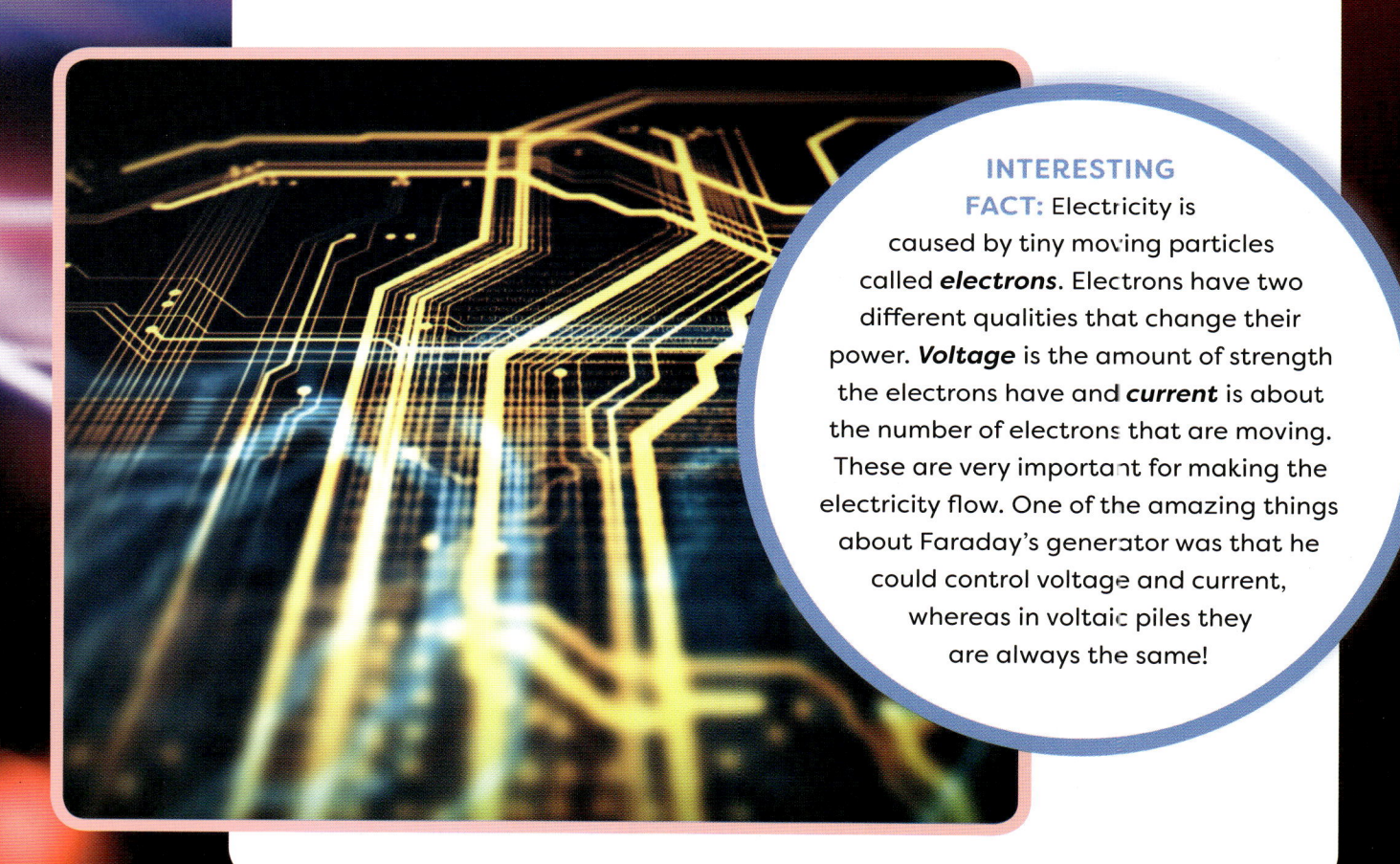

Voltaic Pile.

INTERESTING FACT: Electricity is caused by tiny moving particles called **electrons**. Electrons have two different qualities that change their power. **Voltage** is the amount of strength the electrons have and **current** is about the number of electrons that are moving. These are very important for making the electricity flow. One of the amazing things about Faraday's generator was that he could control voltage and current, whereas in voltaic piles they are always the same!

MAKING ELECTRICITY

Can you imagine a world without electricity? That means no computers, no TV, no phones, no fridges, no cars, no electric lights... and plenty of other things too. Well, only 190 years ago we didn't have any electricity at all!

Benjamin Franklin

In ancient times, people would rub amber with fur to make *static electricity*. Static electricity is the kind of electricity that makes your hair stand up when you rub it with a balloon. But people really became interested in electricity in the 1700s.

INTERESTING FACT: Lightning must have been humans first experience with electricity. Lightning occurs when a huge amount of electrical energy builds up in the clouds. When there's too much electricity for the cloud to hold, the electricity jumps down through the air into the ground and spreads out into Earth. Lightning must have been very important to ancient people, because there were hundreds of different lightning and thunder gods in religions all over the world.

is what Einstein called the combination of all the dimensions in the Universe – not the physical stuff in the universe but the actual space and time. We can use metaphors like the mattress to picture it but really it's beyond our human brain to imagine. Still, physicists like Einstein can use math to describe how and why it works the way that it does.

People today are still trying to dig deeper and answer important questions about gravity. One of the big mysteries is why gravity only works on a big scale, with the objects around you, and planets, and galaxies. But it doesn't seem to have any effect at all on a small scale, with atoms and molecules. Even now scientists all over the world are trying to understand the mysterious and weird force that is gravity. Will you be the one to crack the next clue in the mystery of gravity?

Albert Einstein.

Gravity wells.

Universe Dip

The **dips** that gravity makes in **spacetime** are sometimes shown using pictures like these. Of course, this is not what it *really* looks like, but it helps us to imagine how objects of different weights affect the universe. In the picture below, you can see how heavier and heavier objects make bigger and bigger dips in spacetime, which is represented by the grid. As you can see, something a bit heavy like the Sun, makes a bit of a dip. **Neutron stars** (not really stars, but a very heavy space rock that is sometimes left behind by exploding stars) make a bigger dip. If stars are big enough when they explode, they leave a **black hole** instead. Black holes are some of the heaviest things we've ever found. They are so heavy that even **light** is sucked into them! As you can see, they make the biggest dip of all. Some people think that maybe if you make a deep enough dip, you can actually put a hole in the Universe, making a so-called **wormhole**. What do you think could be on the other side?

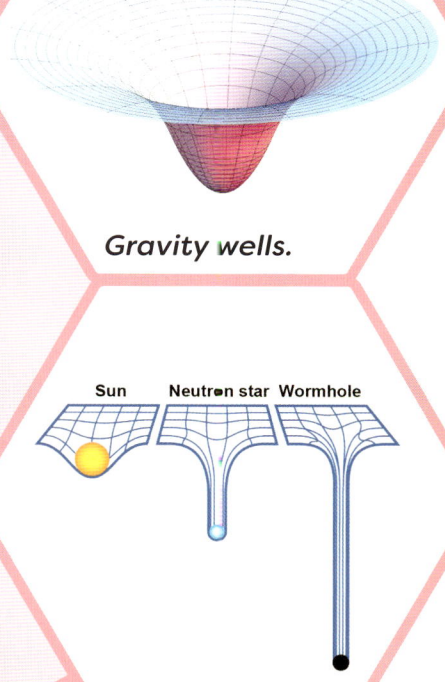

Isaac Newton

The famous English mathematician and oddball named Isaac Newton solved the next piece of the puzzle. In 1687 he published a book which explained the math behind the invisible force he called **gravity**, which made objects move toward each other. His calculations described how everything moved, from the balls in Galileo's experiments, to the planets and the stars. He predicted things that wouldn't be proved for hundreds of years. He even invented a whole new kind of math called **calculus** to make it all work. He changed everything about the way we saw the world and showed that the physical universe could be described with three laws called **the Laws of Motion**. But Newton's theories didn't explain *why* any of it worked the way it did, just *how*.

INTERESTING FACT: Maybe Newton would have done even more, but he was constantly being distracted by his other strange interests. He spent countless hours looking for hidden messages in the Bible and trying to turn lead and other common metals into gold!

Albert Einstein

Albert Einstein came up with the next big step. He was only an office worker in Switzerland at the time! But his theory was so complicated that it took scientists years to really understand it. One way to imagine it is like this...

Picture a mattress in your mind. Put a big heavy object like a bowling ball on the mattress. What happens? Well, the mattress gets a big dip in it where the bowling ball sits. Now imagine that you get a marble and put it on the mattress too. It makes a smaller dip, right? But if you put it too close to the bowling ball then it will roll down towards the bowling ball.

This is a very simplified way of describing how gravity works. The bigger the object, the bigger the dip it makes in spacetime. ***Spacetime***

INTERESTING FACT: Newton was another scientist that studied many different sciences. He also did some important research about light and invented a new kind of telescope. Rather than using lenses, like in Galileo's telescope or a pair of glasses, Newton figured out how to use mirrors instead. His telescope gave the clearest picture yet.

Galileo Galilei

Galileo Galilei was a brilliant Italian scientist, who invented or improved upon all kinds of scientific devices. He also discovered the moons of Jupiter and Venus. He was one of the first people to do experiments using the **scientific method**, the way we do today, using careful tests to see if an idea is correct. He used his method of experimenting to explore the strange power that made things fall to the ground (there was no word for gravity when Galileo did his tests back in the 1500s).

Galileo Galilei.

He carefully measured the time it took for different balls to roll down ramps. He discovered that it didn't matter how heavy the balls were, they all rolled at the same speed!

INTERESTING FACT: Galileo's discovery caused a lot of arguments. 'How can weight not change the speed an object falls?' other scientists argued. 'Does a feather fall as fast as cannonball? Of course not!' Galileo believed that if there was no air then a feather and a cannonball *would* fall at the same speed, but he had no way to prove it. However, when astronauts went to the Moon – where there's almost no air – they dropped a hammer and a feather and proved that Galileo was right: they *did* drop at the same speed!

GRAVITY

What keeps your feet on the ground? What holds the Earth together? What keeps the Earth orbiting around the Sun, and the stars clumped together into galaxies? The answer to all of these things is a weird, invisible force. It is so complicated and strange that only the most brilliant scientists understand it, and even they have unanswered questions. It's called gravity.

It is one of the most powerful and important forces in the universe. It is completely invisible to us! We only know it's there because we can see it working, holding the universe together. Three of the greatest minds in history were needed to unlock the little we know today.

Antennae Galaxies.

INTERESTING FACT: Gravity may not seem like much to you and me. After all, just by jumping your legs are briefly overcoming the gravity of the entire Earth! This is why gravity is called the **weak force**. But you only have to look up into the stars to see the awesome power of gravity. For example, the Antennae galaxies are slowly crashing together! The crash is happening on such a huge scale that to us it doesn't really look like they are moving at all. In fact, they started crashing together about 1.2 billion years ago! But it's all happening because of the unstoppable power of gravity. In about 4 billion years, the same thing is going to happen to us when our galaxy, the **Milky Way**, crashes into the nearest neighboring galaxy, named **Andromeda**.

Dmitri Mendeleev

About eighty years later, more than sixty different elements had been discovered. But nobody could agree on the best way to sort and label them. This was a huge problem, because it stopped many **chemists** from understanding each other's research. Also, nobody understood how they all fit together. It was a strange and complicated puzzle, and there was an international race going on to figure it out.

An English scientist named John Newlands figured out one of the big clues. He realized that there was a repeating pattern in the elements, and they mostly came in groups of eight. He called these groups **octaves** and compared them to notes in a musical scale. Other scientists at the time thought this was so ridiculous that they ignored Newlands important theories!

In the end, Russian chemist Dmitri Mendeleev saw the whole picture. He sorted the table into the groups of eight, then sorted them by atomic weight. **Atomic weight** is the weight of one individual atom. Amazingly, Mendeleev said that wherever there was a gap in his table, the element supposed to fill the gap hadn't been discovered yet!

The Periodic Table is like a map of the atomic world. It shows chemists the huge number of atoms available and tells them how they are going to interact with each other. It is the most important tool available for chemists and chemistry, and it's still growing and changing today. Maybe you will use the Periodic Table to discover an incredible new molecule!

Dmitri Mendeleev.

Antoine-Laurent de Lavoisier

In the 1770s a French nobleman named Antoine-Laurent de Lavoisier took an interest in the elements. Most people at the time were just mixing chemicals together and seeing what happened. Lavoisier's method was much more scientific. Lavoisier and his wife Marie-Anne took exact measurements and did careful experiments in their enormous laboratory – the biggest laboratory in the world at the time. They weren't just trying to discover and sell new substances, they were trying to understand how it all worked.

Lavoisier and his wife.

INTERESTING FACT: One of Lavoisier's biggest discoveries was **the Law of Conservation of Mass**. Lavoisier realized that you can't create or destroy matter – you can just change it from one thing to another.

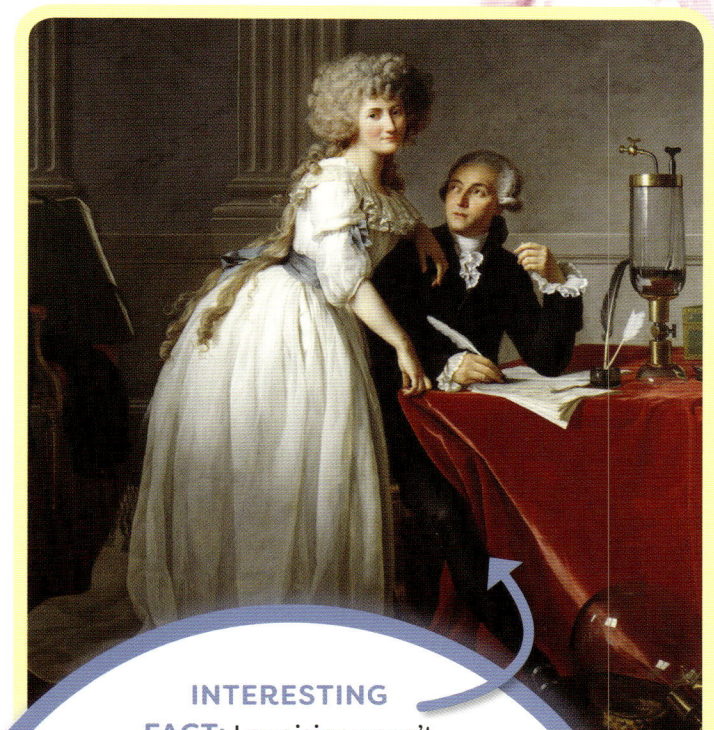

INTERESTING FACT: Lavoisier wasn't just rich, he was super rich. Not many people back in the 1700s had enough money to pay someone to make a giant picture of them and their wife, like this one! Unfortunately, Lavoisier funded his experiments by investing in the company that collected the taxes in France. This company was known for its brutal methods and for keeping all the money for the rich and powerful. Because of this, Lavoisier was one of the thousands of people to be executed during the French Revolution.

e Elements

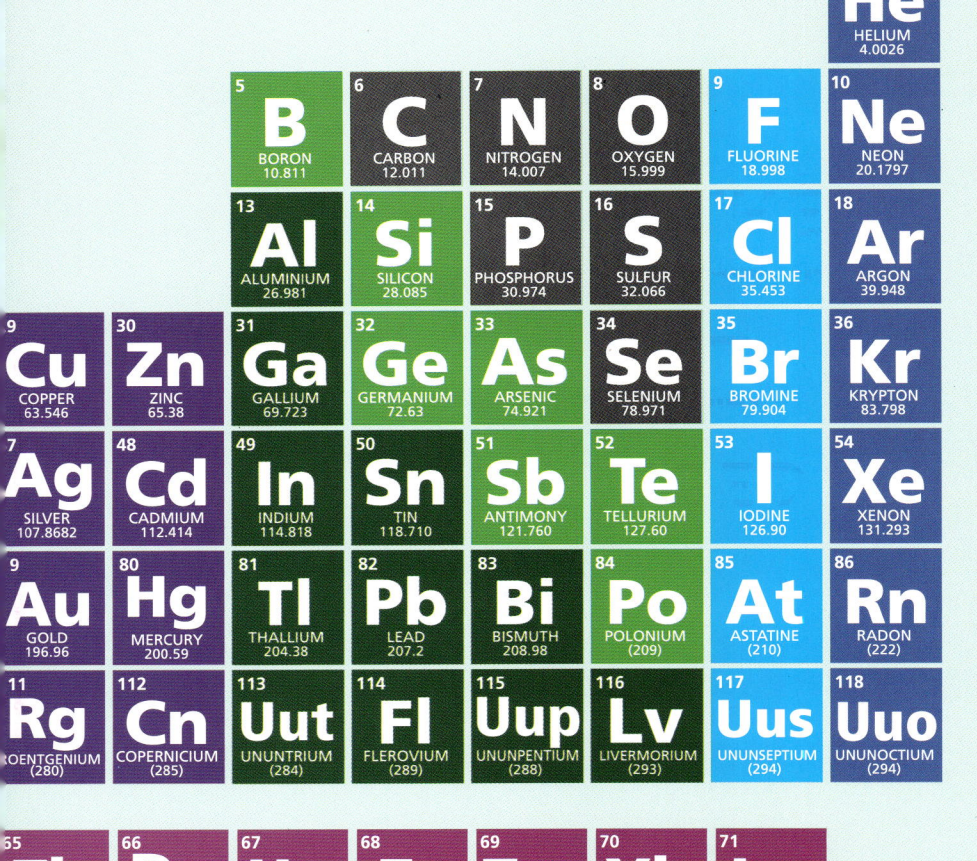

(At), are so rare that scientists think there may be only about 30 grams on Earth. Lots of the others, like Technetium (Tc), don't exist anywhere at all and scientists make them from other elements!

The table even gives you an idea of how the elements will react with one another. All the alkali metals in the first column react very strongly with all the halogens in the second last column. Meanwhile the **noble gases** in the very last column don't react with anything at all!

This is all because the number of protons that an element has also usually decides how many electrons something has. **Electrons** are another type of tiny particle, but they fly around the outside of the atom. When atoms bond together they usually do it by giving, taking or sharing electrons. All the alkali metals have one too many electrons and all the halogens have one too few. That's why they react so well together!

The Periodic Table is the most useful and important tool for chemistry. This is just the start of some of the secrets that it can unlock!

PERIODIC TABLE o

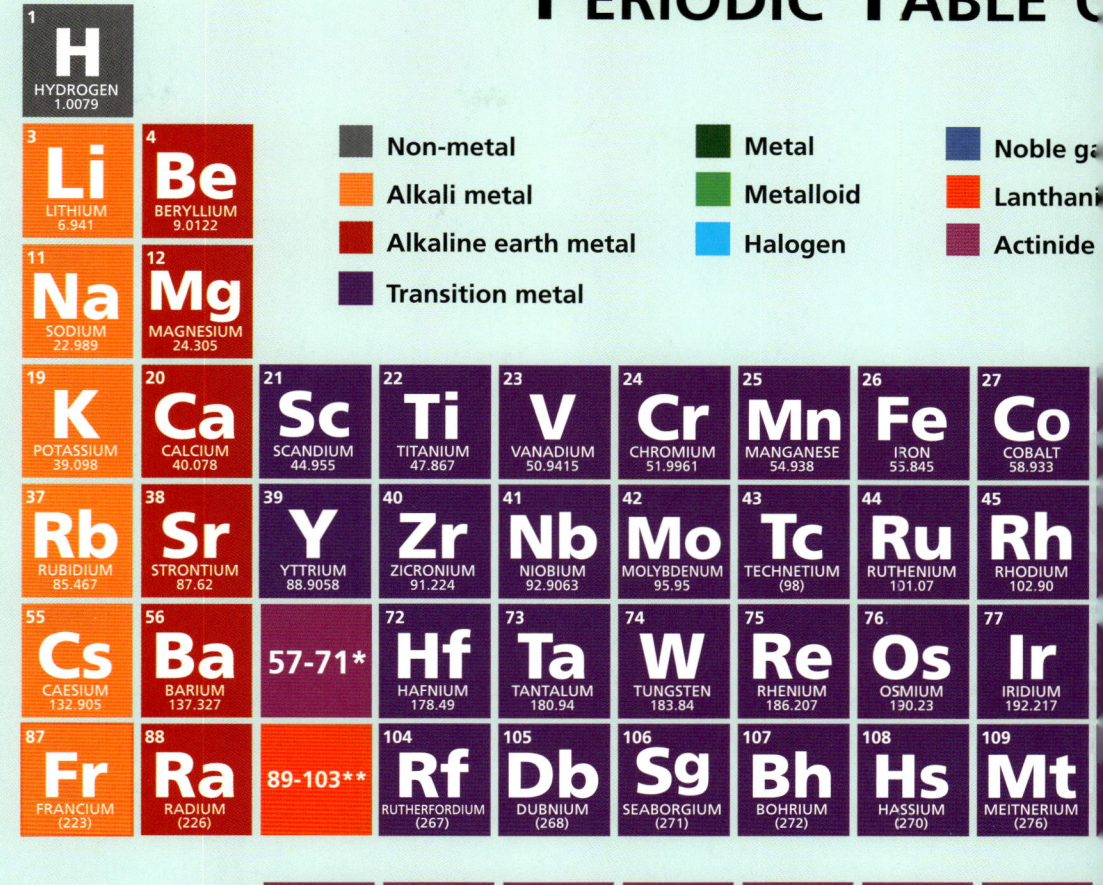

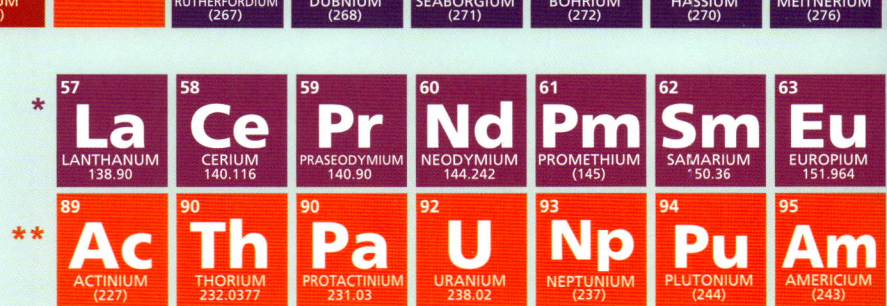

1 H HYDROGEN 1.0079									
3 Li LITHIUM 6.941	**4** Be BERYLLIUM 9.0122								
11 Na SODIUM 22.989	**12** Mg MAGNESIUM 24.305								
19 K POTASSIUM 39.098	**20** Ca CALCIUM 40.078	**21** Sc SCANDIUM 44.955	**22** Ti TITANIUM 47.867	**23** V VANADIUM 50.9415	**24** Cr CHROMIUM 51.9961	**25** Mn MANGANESE 54.938	**26** Fe IRON 55.845	**27** Co COBALT 58.933	
37 Rb RUBIDIUM 85.467	**38** Sr STRONTIUM 87.62	**39** Y YTTRIUM 88.9058	**40** Zr ZICRONIUM 91.224	**41** Nb NIOBIUM 92.9063	**42** Mo MOLYBDENUM 95.95	**43** Tc TECHNETIUM (98)	**44** Ru RUTHENIUM 101.07	**45** Rh RHODIUM 102.90	
55 Cs CAESIUM 132.905	**56** Ba BARIUM 137.327	57-71*	**72** Hf HAFNIUM 178.49	**73** Ta TANTALUM 180.94	**74** W TUNGSTEN 183.84	**75** Re RHENIUM 186.207	**76** Os OSMIUM 190.23	**77** Ir IRIDIUM 192.217	
87 Fr FRANCIUM (223)	**88** Ra RADIUM (226)	89-103**	**104** Rf RUTHERFORDIUM (267)	**105** Db DUBNIUM (268)	**106** Sg SEABORGIUM (271)	**107** Bh BOHRIUM (272)	**108** Hs HASSIUM (270)	**109** Mt MEITNERIUM (276)	

Legend:
- Non-metal
- Alkali metal
- Alkaline earth metal
- Transition metal
- Metal
- Metalloid
- Halogen
- Noble ga...
- Lanthani...
- Actinide

* **57** La LANTHANUM 138.90 | **58** Ce CERIUM 140.116 | **59** Pr PRASEODYMIUM 140.90 | **60** Nd NEODYMIUM 144.242 | **61** Pm PROMETHIUM (145) | **62** Sm SAMARIUM 150.36 | **63** Eu EUROPIUM 151.964

** **89** Ac ACTINIUM (227) | **90** Th THORIUM 232.0377 | **90** Pa PROTACTINIUM 231.03 | **92** U URANIUM 238.02 | **93** Np NEPTUNIUM (237) | **94** Pu PLUTONIUM (244) | **95** Am AMERICIUM (243)

Here's a picture of the Periodic Table that we use today. Every one of letters or pairs of letters is short for a different type of atom. Some of the letters make a lot of sense. 'O' is Oxygen. 'H' is Hydrogen. But some are a bit weird. 'Fe' is Iron! And 'Au' is Gold! That's because they weren't named after the *English* words for iron and gold, but the *Latin* words. Latin is the language that the Romans spoke more than 1,500 years ago.

The table also tells you how many **protons** are each type of atom. Protons are tiny particles that make up atoms. Every atom has a different number of protons. Lithium, or Li, has 3 protons. Lead, or Pb, has 82.

The table tells you all sorts of things. Each of the different colored areas shows elements that are similar to one another. All the purple elements in the middle are called **transition metals**, all the red and orange elements are called **alkali metals** and all the blue elements are called **halogens**. Some of the elements, like Astatine

Hennig Brand

In ancient times people already knew about some types of elements, like copper, gold and carbon, because these were elements that occurred naturally in the world. Ancient peoples also knew how to extract a few elements like iron or sulfur. For thousands of years, people thought they knew all the elements in the world, until along came a German named Hennig Brand.

Brand was not a scientist at all. He was an *alchemist*. Alchemists were people who tried to turn common metals like lead into gold. Today we know that this is a lot of nonsense, but in the 1600s people took it very seriously. Brand thought that maybe urine was a yellow color because it had gold in it! After some weird experiments, he didn't find any gold at all. What he found instead was a brand-new element called *phosphorus*. People ended up paying more for phosphorus than they did for gold anyway!

INTERESTING FACT: Hennig Brand may have found phosphorus by accident rather than on purpose, but lots of scientific discoveries are made by accident. Antibiotics, the microwave oven and x-rays were all discovered by people looking for something else completely! By the way, you can find Phosphorus in the Periodic Table under 'P'.

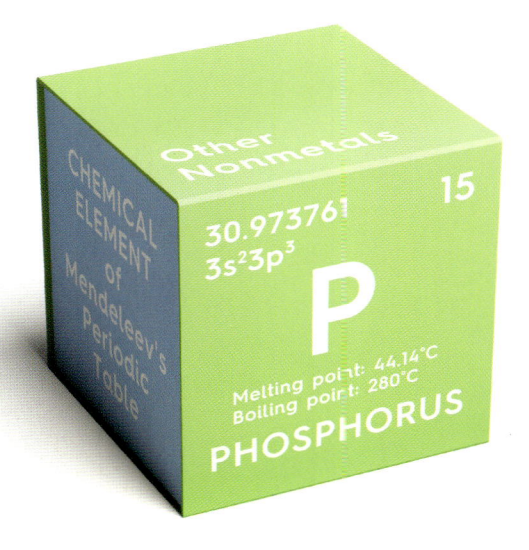

THE PERIODIC TABLE

Imagine you want to build a house on an alien planet. What materials are you going to use? Do they have wood on your new planet? What kind of stone? Do they have clay to make bricks? First of all, you would need to figure out what the building blocks are around you and know how they work together.

Well, when you look at the world of atoms and molecules, it's just like an alien world. **Atoms** are the building blocks that make up every bit of physical matter you can see. When they bond together they make **molecules**. The world of atoms is so tiny that we can't see or even imagine what it's like. Scientists are able to build thousands of molecules to use in medicines, electronics, plastics and so many other things. But first they had to understand the building blocks.

Whenever we have something that's made of only one type of atom, we call it an **element**. One Russian scientist figured out a way to sort the elements that not only described how all they interacted with one another, but also showed people elements nobody even knew about yet. This sorting tool is called the **Periodic Table**.

said that the planets did strange little circles as they went around the Earth, but he couldn't figure out a reason why. People accepted it, even though it didn't make any sense, because they liked putting Earth in the middle so much!

Nicolaus Copernicus

It took another 1,300 years before a Polish astronomer named Nicolaus Copernicus saw that Aristarchus was right all along. He wrote a paper clearly explaining how the planets, including the Earth, moved around the Sun. He made predictions closer than anyone before him. He died shortly afterwards, so he never saw how angry his paper made people. They *hated* it! They did not care that Copernicus' theory made sense, or about the math or science. They were too arrogant to see that the Earth didn't need to be in the center of everything. Many people who agreed with Copernicus were locked in prison or even executed!

Galileo Galilei

Sixty years later, Italian scientist Galileo Galilei used a new invention, the telescope, to look at Jupiter and Venus. He saw that they had their own moons! This was proof that people could see with their own eyes. Not everything in the Universe went around the Earth! Regardless of the evidence, Galileo was *imprisoned for the rest of his life* for suggesting that the Earth was not in the middle.

The solar system.

Aristarchus

Sometimes, the planets move in the opposite direction in the sky, and then they go back to their normal direction. Aristotle's theory didn't explain why. Aristarchus, another Greek philosopher living at the same time, saw that the movement of the planets only made sense if you put the Sun in the middle instead of the Earth. Unfortunately, he was not as famous as Aristotle, so his theory was mostly ignored...for almost 2,000 years!

Jupiter's Moons

This picture shows the moons of Jupiter. They orbit around Jupiter, just like our Moon orbits around Earth, and the Earth orbits around the Sun. Can you imagine how exciting it must have been for Galileo to look through his telescope and see these moons for the first time ever? How would you like to be a scientist who sees something for the first time, that no human has ever seen before?

Eventually people saw sense and accepted the **heliocentric** (meaning 'Sun in the center') theory. Now they understood where the Earth was in the solar system, and it changed the way they thought about the Universe. The Earth did not *have* to be in the middle! But it took 2,000 years of scientists fighting for the truth against people's pride and foolishness. Do you think you could fight for science like Galileo or Aristarchus?

Ptolemy

Ptolemy was another famous Greek philosopher. He lived in Rome almost 500 years after Aristotle and Aristarchus. He also did all kinds of science, including making a new version of Aristotle's theory. He

INTERESTING FACT:

Whenever something small goes around something bigger in space, it is in 'orbit'. We call the smaller object a *satellite*. There are now thousands of human-made satellites orbiting around the Earth. Sometimes a satellite can go around and around for a long time without getting any closer or further away. But often the orbit only lasts for a little while before the big and small objects crash together or fly apart. Satellites crash into the Earth all the time! The Moon is Earth's largest natural satellite. It is a satellite that's almost as old as the Earth itself. But it won't be around forever. Very, very slowly, the moon is getting further and further away from the Earth, about 1.5 inches (4 centimeters) every year. That's about the same speed your fingernails grow!

THE SOLAR SYSTEM

Have you ever looked up at the sky and wondered where we are in the Universe? How do all those stars and planets move around us? Well, people have been looking up at the stars and wondering for a long time what it all means, how it all works, and where they fit into it. Scientists decided to figure it out. But sometimes they had to argue for the truth even when the whole world was against them.

Aristotle

Aristotle was an ancient Greek philosopher living more than 2,300 years ago. He was one of the first people to prove that the world was round, not flat. But he wasn't perfect! He also said that everything in the Universe went around *the Earth* in big circles that we now call **orbits**. This made perfect sense to him. He just assumed that the Earth was the center of the Universe because that was where he lived.

Aristotle And Plato

Remember that famous philosopher Socrates and his students, who we talked about in the previous chapter? Well, Socrates' most famous student was named Plato, who is on the left in this picture. Plato had many students of his own, and the most famous of those was Aristotle, who is standing on the right! This painting is from the 1500s and is called a **fresco**, which means it was painted straight onto a wall. Of course, the painter did not know what Plato or Aristotle really looked like, so do you know who he used instead? Plato's face in this painting is based on the face of another famous scientist who lived at the time: Leonardo da Vinci!

Alhazen

Ibn al-Haytham, known as 'Alhazen' in English, was a Muslim scientist who lived in Iraq about a thousand years ago, about 1,500 years after Socrates. Alhazen was one of the first people to come up with something close to the scientific method. He did it over 500 years before anyone else! He used his method to make important discoveries about light and how we see it.

Alhazen said that you can't *know* how something works without data to prove it. And Alhazen never made up data or used data from places he didn't trust. Mostly he went looking for his own data and recorded it truthfully even if it seemed wrong. He saw the value in testing and retesting, looking for flaws in his theories to make them better.

This is where science really began. You have an idea and then you test it. Then other people need to go and do the same thing. Every time your idea matches the evidence, it is more and more likely to be the correct answer. It is using this incredibly simple but powerful ***scientific method*** that all of the world's science has been discovered. And if you ever do any science then *you* will use it too!

Thinking In Circles

This picture shows one interpretation of the scientific method. First you **observe** the world. Second you come up with a **question**. Next you say what you *think* the answer is – this starting guess is called a **hypothesis**. Then you do an **experiment** or test to check to see if your guess is correct. Then you **analyze** your experiment to see what *really* happened. And finally, you come up with a **conclusion** where you decide if you were right or wrong. Then, with all your new information, you start all over again! Science is something that keeps on going, on and on. Every time you learn something, you ask a new question about what you learned. Why did that happen? How does that work? What does it all mean? That's why this picture is a circle. Long ago and long into the future, the wheel of science and discovery will keep going around and around and around…

SCIENTIFIC METHOD

Socrates and his students.

Most people just know about one part of science, which is collecting **data**. This just means looking at the world and recording what you see. But the second part of science is possibly the most important part. Science is not just about assuming or believing. With science, it doesn't matter what you believe. For a long time, people believed that the Earth was flat, but that didn't make it true! Science needs a special kind of thinking called the **scientific method**.

The scientific method is all about testing, not just guessing. You can't really know something is true unless you test your ideas. If your ideas pass the test, then they aren't totally wrong but they may not be quite right. If anyone anywhere can put your ideas to a test that they don't pass, then you need to make the ideas better.

Socrates and his students

Socrates was an ancient Greek philosopher. Although we don't have any of his own writings, many of his students went on to become famous philosophers too and wrote down what he said.

Socrates invented a way of thinking called the **Socratic method**. Socrates said that if you have a big question, you should break it down into smaller questions. Eventually you have questions small enough that you know the answers. Then you can put all your answers together until the answer to the big question becomes clear. Importantly, the Socratic method needs a group working together. They all learn from one another and discuss the solutions together. This was one of the first times that someone tried to create a way to think better.

Socrates asked lots of questions that many people didn't like. Eventually it got him into trouble. The government of Athens decided that he asked too many questions and executed him!

human. They make us special. Science is a big part of what makes humans different from any other creature on Earth.

Even though science has always been important, it's more dangerous today than ever before. We can now use science to destroy ourselves completely. So, it's more important than ever for everybody to know how science works and how to think like a scientist. We might accidentally create a deadly illness with no cure. Or we might drop nuclear bombs with the power to destroy whole countries. Even today, humans are changing the Earth's atmosphere so that it might become too hot and wild to live.

But science is also the way forward. Science has helped us to travel into space and to look into the distant past. We use science to cure many illnesses and to harness the power of electricity and the atom. It has saved all our lives over and over and over again. Maybe *you* will use science someday to *change* the world, or maybe to *save* the world.

This book is all about the science that we have developed. Some of it we learned 2,000 years ago, and some of it we learned yesterday. This book will tell you about why it's important and how it Changed the World!

INTRODUCTION

Some people say that we live in a world of technology. They say that we live in the Age of Science, like the Bronze Age or the Dark Ages.

This is wrong. We are no more 'scientific' now than at any other time. Sure, we know more today than ever before, but *this has always been true.* Two hundred years ago they had more knowledge than ever before that! And two hundred years from now, there will be more knowledge than today.

When the Roman Empire collapsed, Europe forgot so much about science. But at the same time, algebra was being invented in the Middle East. China was in a golden age of agriculture and construction. India had an explosion of philosophy and language. Polynesian people were exploring islands that Europeans wouldn't see for more than a thousand years.

There is no Age of Science, because humans have *always* been scientists. Technology, discovery, language, learning, numbers, tools, logic – these are all a part of science. They are also what makes us

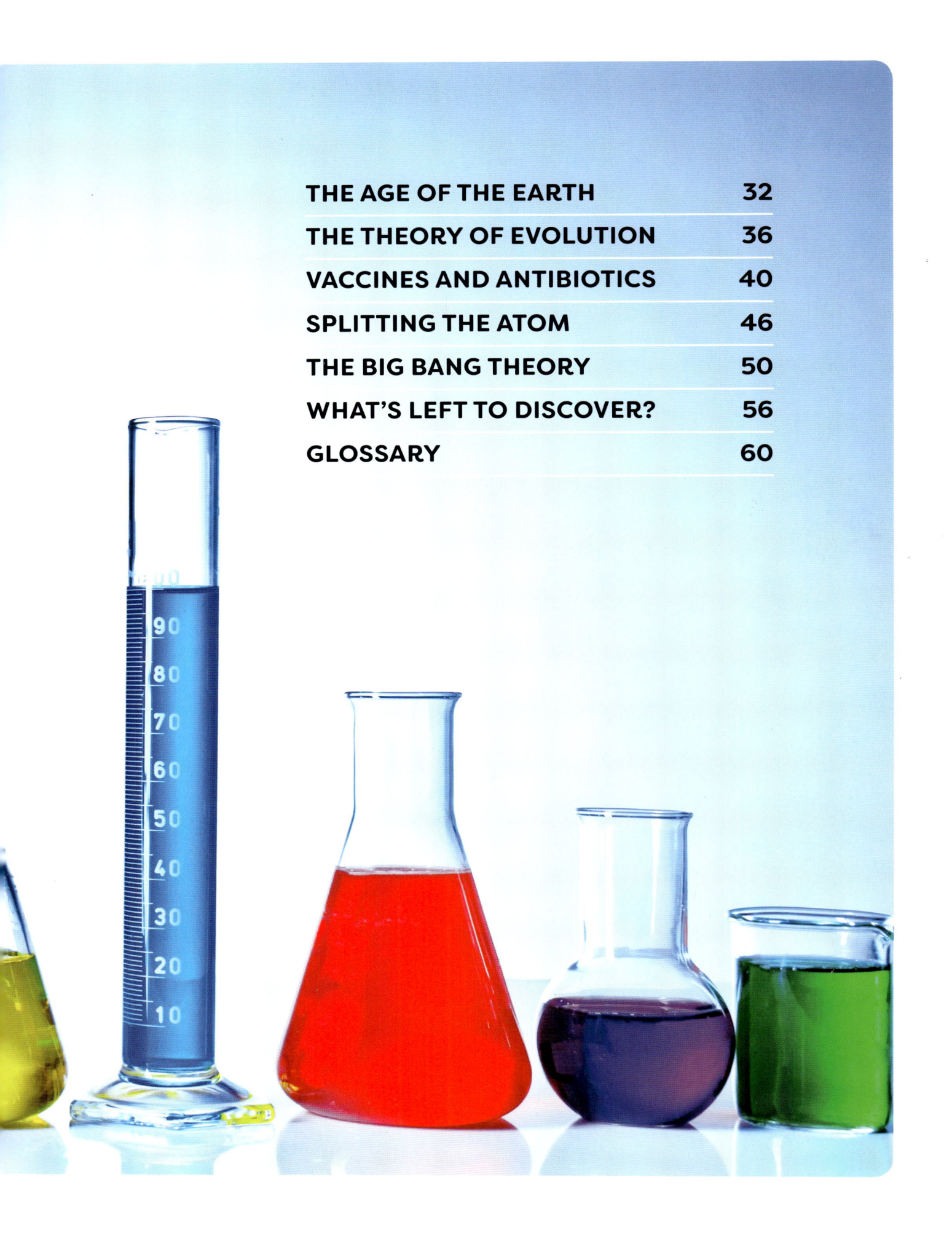

THE AGE OF THE EARTH	**32**
THE THEORY OF EVOLUTION	**36**
VACCINES AND ANTIBIOTICS	**40**
SPLITTING THE ATOM	**46**
THE BIG BANG THEORY	**50**
WHAT'S LEFT TO DISCOVER?	**56**
GLOSSARY	**60**

Contents

INTRODUCTION	6
SCIENTIFIC METHOD	8
THE SOLAR SYSTEM	10
THE PERIODIC TABLE	14
GRAVITY	20
MAKING ELECTRICITY	24
FLIGHT	28

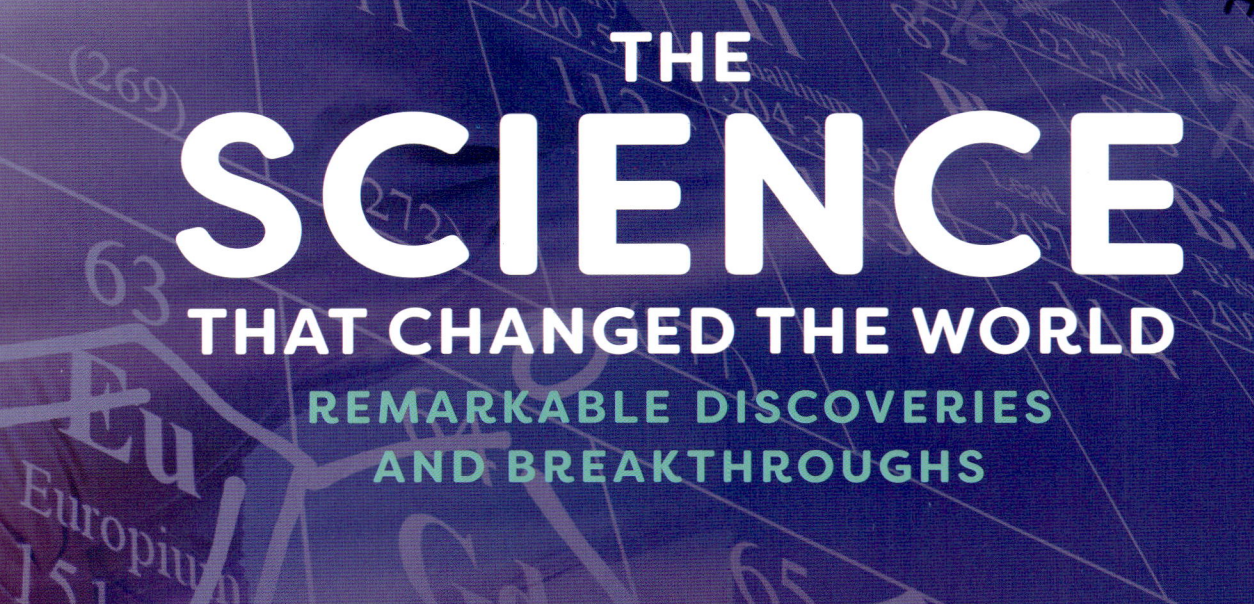

THE SCIENCE
THAT CHANGED THE WORLD
REMARKABLE DISCOVERIES AND BREAKTHROUGHS

Stuart Kumar-Terry

young reed

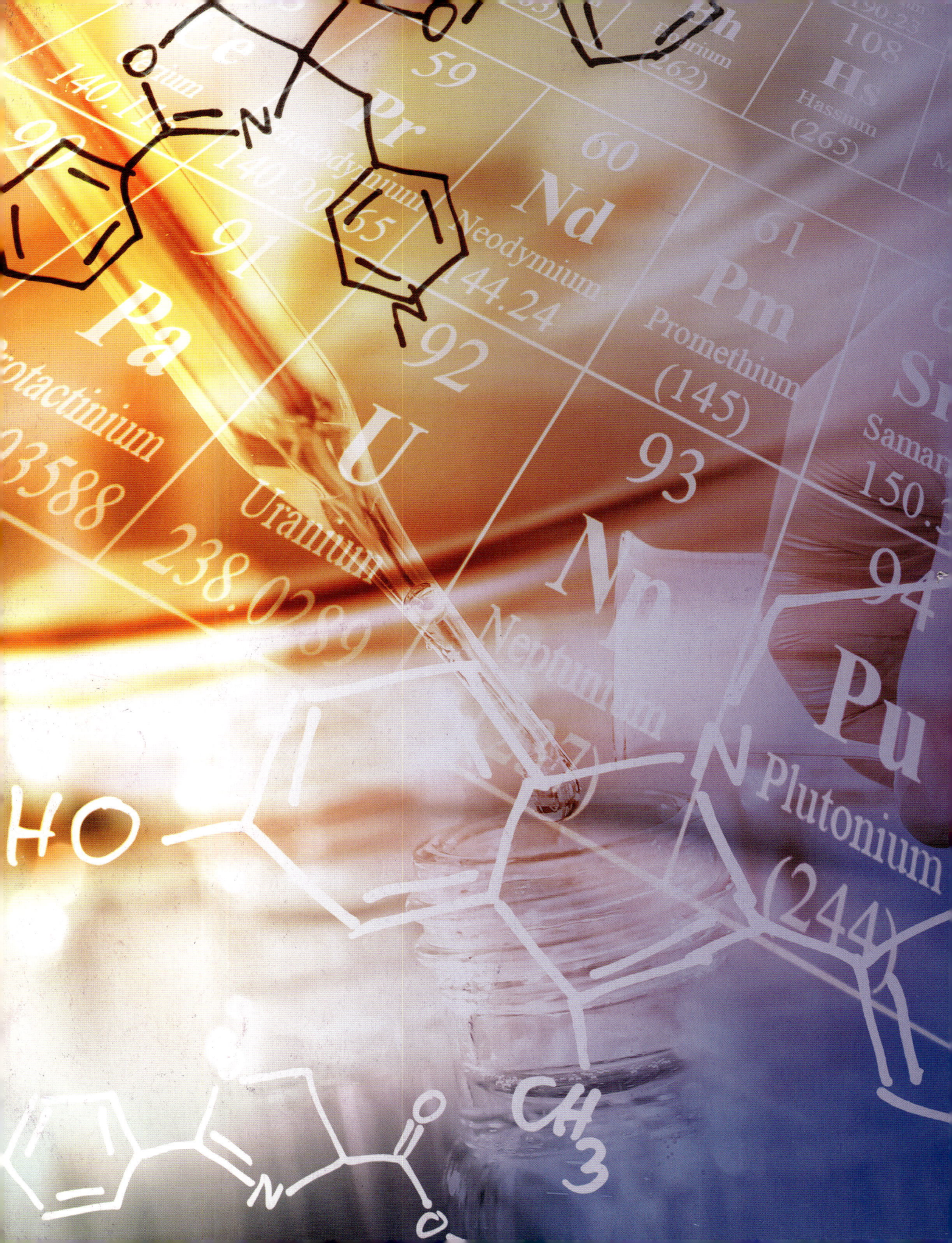

THE SCIENCE
THAT CHANGED THE WORLD